The
Southern Way

The regular volume for the Southern devotee

Kevin Robertson

Issue 47

ISBN 9781909328884

First published in 2019 by Noodle Books
an imprint of Crécy Publishing Ltd

New contact details
All editorial submissions to:
The Southern Way (Kevin Robertson)
'Silmaril'
Upper Lambourn
Hungerford
Berkshire RG17 8QR
Tel: 01488 674143
editorial@thesouthernway.co.uk

A CIP record for this book is available from the British Library

Publisher's note: Every effort has been made to identify and correctly attribute photographic credits. Any error that may have occurred is entirely unintentional.

Printed in the UK by Latimer Trend

Noodle Books is an imprint of
Crécy Publishing Limited
1a Ringway Trading Estate
Shadowmoss Road
Manchester M22 5LH

www.crecy.co.uk

Issue No 48 of THE SOUTHERN WAY
ISBN 9781909328891
available in October 2019 at £14.95

To receive your copy the moment it is released, order in advance from your usual supplier, or it can be sent post-free (UK) direct from the publisher:

Crécy Publishing Ltd

1a Ringway Trading Estate, Shadowmoss Road, Manchester M22 5LH

Tel 0161 499 0024

www.crecy.co.uk

enquiries@crecy.co.uk

Front cover:
A survivor. 'West Country' No. 34095, formerly carrying the name *Brentor*, outside the lift road at the front of Eastleigh shed and temporarily minus its tender. No date, and to be fair a bit care-worn as well, witness the patch on the lower right of the cab side-sheet, but she is still in service and would remain as such until the very end in July 1967. *Bob Winkworth*

Rear cover:
Southern architecture. Lymington Town station. *Roger Holmes*

Title page:
Marchwood station (referred to in the letter by Michael Upton on page 85), seen here with a special DEMU service. In the distance the line continues to Hythe and Fawley, but as Michael points out, it is all currently basically in hibernation, although there remain persistent rumours of a resurgence at least as far as Hythe. The diminutive signal box is built into the structure of the station building and is identified as the rectangular extension on to the platform with the green/white station name underneath. Standard SR concrete post lighting is *in situ* and it will be noted the loop on what is a single line is also signalled for bi-directional running with mechanical signals. We think it remains as such today, even in its mothballed state.

Contents

Introduction

First of all, welcome to the latest edition of *Southern Way*. If you are a long-suffering reader, thank you for staying the course; if you are new to us, a very warm welcome. For my part, I probably have the most enjoyable job of all in that I get to see everything ahead of publication as well as having the (terrible) job of being able to dive into several archives in search of images and material generally – well, somebody has to do it.

I hope too that for this issue, and with the *SW* series having also been in existence for more than twelve years now, I can take this opportunity to include three articles that I might have held back through necessity in earlier times.

Let me say straight away that this is absolutely NO reflection on the individual compilers. All three have diligently researched what are really most interesting subjects but they come with one particular thread in common, and that is a lack of contemporary illustrations.

Now years ago one of my personal gripes was to see a branch line/railway history with an illustration showing not the actual location referred to but, '… a view similar to …', or. '… this is taken not at … but at a totally (unrelated) location …' Indeed, I recall discussing this with Paul Karau in the early days of Wild Swan Publishing and he agreed with me – and I think we all have to admit Paul changed the face of railway publishing considerably from 1979 onwards.

So where are the problems in this issue? Well, as I say, they are not really problems and certainly not with the literary content of the actual articles; but I know we all like photographs and, simply put, where does one find contemporary illustrations to go with 'Wallers Ash' in the 1840s, 'Happenstance', and even contemporary 'Slip coaches on the South Eastern'? The answer is simply that they may not even exist, hence what there is within this issue may not be perhaps quite the same number of photos of the subjects that we would normally like to include. So do please bear with us – we, and the compilers, have tried everything that is feasible. And that does indeed bring me to another point – *feasibility*.

If you as a reader scour the various railway photo sites, museum collections both national and local, and even the worldwide photo archives, there are still literally thousands of railway images out there. Unfortunately though the costs of publishing these are sometimes prohibitive. I am deliberately not mentioning figures or organisations here as many are indeed most helpful, but to obtain, and I use this purely as an example, a single slip-coach view could involve hundreds of miles of travel, with it the associated cost, and then perhaps a three-figure fee for permission to use that one view. I am sorry, we simply do not run to those amounts.

Away though from the shopping basket; and what I am proud about with this issue is we do have two South Eastern area articles! So we made it! I cannot guarantee the same balance will be maintained in future because the following pages are, in consequence, a bit 'light' on the LBSCR side. What I can assure you is that trying to sit on the fence and keep everyone happy is not easy. (My proof reader evidently agrees with me as he adds 'I always think it's bl**dy painful!')

Finally for now, I had the pleasure a few weeks ago of travelling on the former GWR main line into Paddington and then the former SECR lines out of Charing Cross – all 'work' related. (Yes even the GWR was a pleasure – I say that with a degree of trepidation considering our reader profile, of course.) I had been on both routes in the winter, but there and back in darkness is not ideal for observation so a daylight run was eagerly anticipated.

My goodness how things have changed. New railway infrastructure development almost everywhere you look. It might not be '4-CORs, 'Schools', 'Hastings Units', or even 'Blue Pullman' sets out of Paddington, (the latter the other major project I am currently working on), but it is still a railway that is growing. It is also clean and efficient, and I have to say all the trains ran to time. Yes, of course, I would rather view the past but I do still enjoy the present and so it appears do others, as witness spotters at several locations *en route*. Long may it continue, for if it were to stop it may mean we could eventually run out of things to write about!

Kevin Robertson

Our long-time friend Roger Simmonds sent this view in with a puzzler. Fortunately we got it right – so over to you. The questions being: What feature of this former LSWR signal box had been modified/removed from most other surviving LSWR signal boxes of this particular design by the 1960s? Our immediate answer was the covering up of the once ornate external cross-bracing that was a feature of this design below the windows, but it was quickly discovered said timber planks were an addition dating from Southern days. The answer instead is the removal of the timber valance at the top of the windows, Sidmouth Junction being one of the last to retain this distinctive LSWR style. The support to the access steps looks none too strong either. The other signalman's essentials are all present; a goodly supply of coal for the stove and even the luxury of an outdoor privy – what more could a man ask for?

Another Bob Winkworth view, this time the renowned 'B4' No. 30096, which managed to outlive steam on the main line by being sold out of service to work for Messrs Corral's at industrial Southampton. As such she could often be seen trundling alongside the BR routes south of Northam Junction until a second reprieve and a permanent home on the Bluebell Railway.

Disaster at Waller's Ash Tunnel

Stephen Duffell

'Dreadful, melancholic, frightful, calamitous', were just some of the terms the newspapers of the time used to describe an accident in which four men died. Waller's Ash Tunnel lay on the London and South Western Railway between Winchester and Andover Road station (renamed Micheldever in 1854), and trains had been passing through it for a couple of years since the opening of the line.

A contemporary report states, 'On Saturday 2 April 1842, men were working in the tunnel and others were in a shaft above the arch, when a fall of chalk hurled men down to the bottom of the shaft, breaking the tunnel arch and burying them in debris, killing four.' The newspaper reports, mainly in the *Hampshire Chronicle*, and subsequent inquest into the deaths revealed the whole sorry story:

First indications of a problem in the tunnel occurred four to six weeks before the collapse when a soft chalky substance was seen dripping from the roof of the tunnel, some 30 feet in from the Winchester portal (the south end). Then two weeks before, the surface of the earth over this particular place was found to be giving way – a shaft had been made at this spot during the tunnel's construction which was not completely filled in. During construction it had not been deemed prudent to fill up this shaft beyond a certain height, the upper portion being left open until the lower should have become consolidated. About a week before, a slip of chalk fell from off the sides of this shaft, which was observed by the inspector of the district; and on the Tuesday before, an examination took place by the engineers of the line with orders given to reopen the shaft and remove the material around it. This process was then commenced and a very considerable portion of the super-incumbent weight had been removed. During this period no perceptible change of the arch took place; but on Saturday morning early, the part of the arch immediately beneath the shaft gave symptoms of motion; and, although the watchman below communicated this fact to the workmen above, they still continued their operations, and in about an hour were unfortunately precipitated, with a quantity of loose chalk, into the tunnel. Six of the number were buried: and of these two were taken out unhurt, whilst the others met their death.

The men had started their shift at 6 am and those originally in the shaft were James Watmore aged 58 years, his two sons, one 30 years and the other 18, Charles Nyas aged 20, James Allett, James Batchelor aged 19, Thomas Batchelor aged 25, Daniel Laws 23, William Knight 24 and John Gambell. Nothing particular was observed, until ten minutes to eight o'clock, when they were talking about going to breakfast. At this moment, as Gambell describes it, the place about them began to close in like a whirlpool, and Watmore, Nyas, Allett and James Batchelor were hurled into the abyss beneath, some 40 to 50 feet, the tunnel below giving way to a distance of about 30 feet, and hurled them amongst the immense mass of falling material. Laws, T Batchelor, Knight, and one of the sons of Watmore, fell from a considerable height, and the two first were so severely injured as to be obliged to be removed to Winchester Hospital, where they were promptly attended to by Mr Lightfoot, the surgeon. Gambell states that he must have immediately shared the fate of the four unfortunate men who had been crushed to death, had he not fortunately got hold of a piece of rope which hung from the scaffolding: but on this giving way, he fell a depth of 40 feet and received a severe hurt in the spine, had his right cheek, arms and hands severely lacerated by the rough material or chalk stone in his fall, and was carried home to his father's residence at Micheldever, where he at present lies.

The alarm of the unfortunate calamity was soon given and reached Andover Road station, where the porters and men employed there were instantly despatched to the assistance of the sufferers. After the removal of Gambell, Laws, Knight and Thomas Batchelor, and the two younger Watmores, a number of workmen began digging out the other unfortunate sufferers. The first found was Allett who was in a standing position, with his head and almost every bone in his body smashed to pieces. The next was Nyas, who was also frightfully mutilated; the third, poor old Watmore, recovered after four hours labour, and who presented a sorry spectacle; and the last was James Batchelor.

'Their remains were taken to a small hut over the tunnel, where they stayed until the coroner's inquest. A medical gentleman, residing on the vicinity of Mitchel Devon (sic) was in attendance at the spot a few minutes after the accident, and rendered the most prompt and humane attention to the unfortunate sufferers. Those in the shaft were:

James Watmore, a married man with a large family, aged 58 – dead

Thomas Batchelor, aged 19, single man – dead

Charles Nyas, aged 20, single man – dead

James Allett, single man, aged 23 – dead

James Batchelor, aged 25, taken to Winchester Hospital – head, face, legs and other parts of his body seriously contused, considered in a dangerous state

David Laws, a single man aged 24, also taken to Winchester Hospital – seriously injured and in a dangerous state

Thomas Knight, aged 24, recently married – head, back and other parts of his body severely bruised, not dangerous

John Campbell 22 – injured in the same manner as Knight, not in danger

Both the sons of Watmore, with only a few bruises

The inquest starts

The inquest was held on the following Monday, 4 April, at the 'Cart and Horses' Inn at Kings Worthy, at 11 o'clock on the morning. The coroner was Mr Todd and when the 12 jury men appeared they were chiefly labourers, some wearing smockfrocks. The Coroner, however, without waiting to have their names called, said he was extremely sorry to have to commence his duty by making a public complaint of the conduct of an officer of his court. He had given the most explicit injunctions to the constable to summon the most respectable jury that could be collected in the neighbourhood. He had no fault to find with any of those who had attended as jurors, all of them were no doubt, respectable enough for their station, and some might very properly be selected for such an investigation; but there were others whom it would be positively cruel to call upon to take part in these proceedings. Persons in smockfrocks and pensioners really should not be expected to share the responsibility of this case. It demanded the utmost attention and most careful consideration of men of some education, independence and station in the county. The eyes of the whole kingdom were fixed upon them; the public took a very great interest in the progress and result of their proceedings and he would not take on himself the responsibility of conducting the inquiry alone. He would therefore discharge the present jury and immediately issue another warrant, requiring the constable to summon a class of persons more independent in station and character. He begged them to believe that he adopted this course only under a deep feeling of positive duty, and without the slightest disrespect to any of them individually. He felt that in a case of so much importance it was necessary that he should have the assistance of gentlemen of independent property and station, persons in the habit of travelling by railways, and possessing, from education and habits of life, the means of forming an intelligent judgement upon the whole facts submitted to them. If he could not have independent gentlemen he must have respectable tradesmen; he could not go lower than that.

(He wouldn't half get stick for that, these days. I suspect, though, that in the days before any form of compulsory education, he might have had something of a point, though I also suspect that he probably underestimated the capabilities of the first-chosen jury. I would think the circumstances very similar to the call that there has been to do away with juries in complicated fraud cases, where laymen are deemed to be unlikely to be able to understand the financial complexity of the matter. – Ed)

Seen from the top of the northern portal of Wallers Ash, a down Bournemouth line service will soon be entering the tunnel. Chalk falls are a regular feature of the railway between Winchester and Basingstoke with evidence in the cess, particularly on the down side. *S.C. Townroe*

It was particularly annoying to him to have to make these observations; but it would be injustice to his own feelings and office, it would be unfair to the public, it would be cruel to those whom he addressed, to expect such persons to share in the responsibility of this enquiry. He did not shrink from his own fair portion; but he would not, through the carelessness or ignorance of a constable, consent to proceed without a better and a more numerous jury. Persons of the humbler class of life would be placed in the most awkward predicament in having to pronounce a verdict, and probably something more, in a case of such magnitude. The present jury were now discharged. He should have no objection that some of them should be re-summoned; and as to the others he should take care that their 'shilling' should be paid them if the money came out of his pocket. He regretted that any delay should intervene; it was no fault of his, however, for he had given the most particular injunctions on the subject to the constable. The whole conduct of that officer had been most reprehensible. Owing to his neglect, he himself had received no notice of the case till 12 hours after everybody else knew of it. He had directed himself not to confine himself to one parish, but to summon a respectable jury from the whole neighbourhood. The manner in which he had discharged that duty showed that he was no more fit to be a constable than a lord chancellor. If he had it in his power, he should certainly fine him £5, and if he did not, within reasonable time, summon a more respectable jury, he should indict him at the present sessions.

After the lapse of about an hour and a half the following jury, consisting of respectable persons of the county, were sworn: Samuel Devon, Richard Vokes, William Levitt, Thomas Turner, Robert Gandy, William Chalwin, Charles Robinson, Robert Hammond, George Paine, Robert Taplin, Thomas Watson, Michael Vokes (foreman), Charles Allen, Noah Vincent, Thomas Taylor, and John Tomkins.

Duties of the jury

The coroner, addressing the jury, said they were aware that the case which they were about to investigate was one of considerable importance, and excited much interest in the public mind. Great responsibility was, therefore, thrown upon them, and he should have to beg their best attention, in order to enable them to form a correct conclusion from the facts laid before them. The oath they had just taken sufficiently indicated the nature of the inquiry. So far as it spoke of the cause of death, regular proof from the medical witnesses he had summoned would be given, so that they would have a foundation for every part of their verdict. That portion of the inquiry would not take up much time. The incidental matters, however, connected with the death of these unfortunate men were of the greatest importance, and must engage their closest attention. Very competent witnesses would be called to prove everything that had transpired before and at the time of the accident; and he trusted the whole of the circumstances would be brought before them. It would not be proper for him to anticipate the evidence or allude to any of the reports which might have reached their ears, except so far as to beg of them to dismiss such matters

entirely from their minds. Any information they might possess might guide them in putting questions to witnesses, but their verdict must be founded on statements received on oath.

Their first duty was to take a view of the bodies and of the place where the calamity had occurred. They should then return and hear such evidence as might satisfy their minds as to the cause and manner of the accident. The bodies which lay in a small house near the tunnel appropriated for labourers on the line, presented a much less shocking spectacle than might have been expected. Indeed, their appearance was more that of persons who had died of suffocation than contusion or mutilation. The jury did not return to the 'Cart and Horses' till half-past two.

The labourers give evidence

The first witness to give evidence was Mr. H. Lyford, a surgeon from Winchester. He was called on Saturday morning about 8 o'clock, to attend the accident at the Waller's-ash tunnel. He went by train from Winchester, and on his way met with two men who were being conveyed to Winchester on a truck. He stopped and examined them. One had a fractured collar bone and appeared in a very collapsed state and he directed that they should be conveyed to the hospital without delay. I proceeded a short distance to Capon's cottage by the side of the railway, where the four bodies were lying. I saw a young man dead, on whose body were very few marks of injury, and the general appearance of the corpse conveyed to his mind the idea that he had died from suffocation.

He then went on to the tunnel where a great number of men were digging for bodies supposed to be buried, the tunnel itself at the southern extremity being full of chalk, which had fallen in. He saw one dead body dug out, and left the labourers searching for the others. He had since seen the bodies of four men now lying in the cottage, and on the whole they all presented a similar appearance having very little external contusion, and bearing the marks of death by suffocation, which I am of the opinion was the immediate cause of death in each case.

Having established the cause of death, the remaining witnesses explained the circumstances of the accident, starting with the foremen in charge of the night-shift labourers. George Price of Basingstoke was a railway ganger and supervised a gang of men set to work on the top of Waller's Ash tunnel, beginning on the Wednesday night, directed by Mr. Ogilvie, an engineer employed under Mr. Brassey, the contractor.

His duty was to look after the men who were removing the chalk, some 20 to 30 feet deep, from the top of the brickwork. When he first got there, he saw the brickwork from the inside; at the top of the tunnel it was a little cracked and sunk, and along both sides just at the spring of the arch. There was, originally, a hollow space above the arch, and it is supposed this sinking was occasioned by a portion of the soil above having fallen in. There did not appear to me to be any danger. He had 23 men employed in removing the chalk. They continued working all Wednesday and every succeeding night, another gang being employed during the day. A great quantity of chalk was removed, and no change took place in the state of the brickwork till Saturday morning between 3 and 4 o'clock. At that time the watchman came up to George Price and said he thought there was something amiss for he saw little bits of brick dropping. Price then paid particular attention to the state of the arch and saw small pieces of brickwork chipping off and falling faster than he had seen before. This chipping continued to increase for half an hour, and then as much as a wheel-barrow full fell from one spot to the thickness of half a brick. He immediately sent a watchman to Winchester to inform Mr. Douglas, the inspector of the line. Price then went to the top of the tunnel and got every one of them out of the hole for fear anything would happen. It was then about 4 o'clock, and there were no men at work in the tunnel. The men were put to work on another job, and Price went down below to see what state the tunnel was in. In about 10 minutes as much as three or four wheel-barrows-fulls had fallen from the brickwork, extending to a greater depth. He sent another messenger to Winchester to say it was getting worse, fearing the former would not make enough alarm. He did so to stop the trains at Winchester. He

remained by himself till about a quarter to six, when Henry Ferris, the day foreman, came, followed by several other labourers, it being nearly their time to begin work.

During the interval from 4 o'clock to 6 the brickwork continued to fall, but not so quickly as before. I wished the men to look at it, and some of the men said they would work in it, and others not. After Henry Ferris has inspected the brickwork he went up with his men to work on the top. Price's men had gone away, but Price remained below till the accident happened. Mr. Thomas Jones, foreman of the miners, arrived between 6 and 7 o'clock, and under his directions several men were employed in shoring up the brickwork with timber. We were so employed till about a quarter to 7 o'clock, when the brickwork began to break in deeper, faster and wider. They kept working till the arch gave way, and the earth began to fall in. At that time there were about a dozen men or more at work inside the tunnel, and about 20 on top. The first fracture of the arch was about a yard square: it continues to increase, followed by

Another Townroe image, this time of a Urie 'S15' literally about to enter the southern portal of the tunnel with a northbound freight. A goodly supply of fuel in the tender but perhaps not to the finest quality. More than a century and half after the fall it is still hard to appreciate that there was scaffolding placed on the down line while they dealt with the fall and yet trains were continuing to pass: working single line, on the up side.

a great quantity of chalk, which continued to fall for nearly a quarter of an hour, when the opening extended nearly 20 or 30 feet in length and the full width of the tunnel. About 12 men who were at work above came down with the chalk soil. None of the men inside were injured as they saw their danger in time to make their escape. I heard the men who were buried in the chalk cry out for about five minutes, 'Oh, Lord!' 'Oh, Christ!' The remainder of the men immediately set to work to dig out the sufferers, and Price proceeded to give notice of what had happened at Andover Road station. He did not know the four men who were killed, as they were Ferris's men.

Henry Ferris was examined next. He lived in Micheldever, near the Andover Road station, was employed on the railway as a ganger, and supervised a gang of 21 men. They started work the previous Monday, with directions to remove the chalk from the top of the tunnel. We worked off and on every day of the week till Friday night, up to which time no change had taken place in the tunnel to attract any notice. About half-past 6 o'clock on Saturday morning he went to work. He saw George Price, foreman of the night gang, under the tunnel, as he passed by on a small truck pushed by George Trendley, one of his men. Ferris observed that a small portion of the brickwork had shelved off to the extent of a couple of barrows-full since the night before; but I did not think from that that there was any danger. Price told Ferris he considered it dangerous and he had taken his men off about 4 o'clock, but did not caution me about placing my men. Ferris went above, got into the hole, and saw no alteration. As Ferris saw no danger he set his men to work as usual. None objected to work, doing so willingly. Ferris saw no change take place before the accident, but the fall was so instantaneous there was no warning and no notion of any danger from below. There was a man sent up, but he had not time to reach us before the fall. Ferris had not been out of the shaft above five or ten minutes when the fall took place. He did not leave the hole because he saw any danger, but got out to fix some posts to make another stage for men to work upon. At the moment the accident happened, Ferris was two or three yards from the edge of the hole. The whole mass appeared to go in at one time, and two of the stages on which the men were working fell in with the chalk and nine or ten of the men. Digging immediately commenced at the top for the men that were buried, and ropes were let down in case others should fall, allowing them to be extricated through the hole, as the tunnel was closed up. Ferris assisted in getting Elliot out, and knew the four dead men, but did not see them all dug out. Ferris agreed in response to a question by a juror that at 6 o'clock Price still adhered to the opinion that there was danger, at least he said he had taken off his men in apprehension of danger.

Next witness was a labourer, William Watmore, who lived at Micheldever, and was the son of James Watmore, who was killed in the tunnel. He was at work in Ferris's gang, on the top stage over the shaft, when the fall took place and saw no danger till the accident happened. None of the men were unwilling to work, and all seemed more willing to go down that morning than he ever saw before. His father was at the bottom of the shaft, which might have been 20 feet deep, and at the top wider than the tunnel. There were about 11 men in the shaft, three at the bottom and the rest on stages. They had no notice of the accident and received no warning. It happened all of a sudden, and none of the men in the shaft called out before it took place. No alarm whatever was given. He and his brother jumped off and saved ourselves, but the other nine fell through with the chalk. The rest of the men immediately set to work to dig them out. He worked till he was ready to drop. The first dug out was Thomas Batchelor, the next Daniel Laws – they were both alive and sensible. They were directly sent to the hospital. The next we dug out was Charles Nyas, quite dead. My father was next taken out dead; then William Elliot and James Batchellor (sic), quite dead. The rest of the men got out themselves without being much hurt. Questioned by a juror about what Ferris had told them of events within the tunnel, Watmore replied that Ferris did not tell them that any bricks had fallen. They did not know when they went to work that anything unusual had occurred in the tunnel. Ferris was tying a rope to a post just opposite our stage not long before the accident – that post also gave way. Some of the men had previously objected to go down the shaft – some objected every day – but none did so on this morning. No beer was given, nor anything else, to induce them to go down. We all went to work over the tunnel, and did not pass through it. The night gang had all gone off before we got there. We did not know they had been taken off in consequence of the danger. We did not hear that any brickwork had fallen.

Another labourer, Charles Knapp, who also lived at Micheldever, was at work in the day gang last Saturday morning when the accident happened. On Friday he was at work on the bottom stage in the shaft. On Saturday morning we were ordered to turn into the hole again. He rather objected because it made his back ache when he worked there the day before; but he was not afraid not having heard of any danger. He did go down the shaft that morning as before; but after a few minutes Ferris ordered James Batchelor to take his place, which he did, and Knapp got out to wheel the stuff away from the top of the tunnel, till the planks on which he wheeled were wanted below so he went to work there a little while. He returned to fetch his shovel, and on returning with it, just as he was entering the tunnel again, he met Mr. Douglas, who said to him, 'You get back as fast as you can and tell the men to get out of the hole'. He ran up the slope directly, but before he could get to the top, it fell in, scaffolding and all. Mr. Douglas did not seem frightened when he spoke to him. He heard nothing till it all fell in together. When he left the tunnel to fetch his shovel, nothing that he knew of had fallen in except a brick or two, and Mr. Jones was then in the tunnel throwing up a brick to see whether any more would fall. There were at this time perhaps 10 or 11 men fixing timber, near Mr. Jones, to support the brickwork of the arch. The first Knapp heard of any danger was from Mr. Douglas. All he saw of danger was the falling in of two or three bricks when Mr. Jones chucked up the piece to test the solidity of the brickwork. He assisted to dig out the men.

The south end tunnel mouth is just visible in the background as No. 35028 *Clan Line* heads south with the 'Bournemouth Belle', 20 February 1960. Note modernisation, in the form of the colour light distant signal for Wallers Ash. *Tony Molyneaux*

The final witness in the afternoon was George Mansbridge, who lived at Kings Worthy, and was employed on the railway in Mr. Capon's gang. He was at work on Saturday morning in the tunnel close under the shaft where the brickwork fell in, assisting to shore it up with planks. He had seen for a quarter of an hour before the accident happened a number of bricks fall, about a barrowful, some whole and some broken, that fell from that part of the arch which afterwards fell in. He heard Mr. Jones tell someone directly after the bricks fell to go and tell the men to get out of the hole. Whether anyone went he did not know. About a quarter of an hour afterwards Thomas Watmore, who was then working in the tunnel, said, 'Why, there is someone working above now;' upon which, Mr. Jones said, 'Go along up to the top and tell them to get out.' He did not know whether anyone went or not, but within a minute or

two the whole mass fell in. No one in the tunnel was hurt. They could see it come as long as two minutes before and had time to escape. The brickwork fell first, the top came in all together, and the chalk followed directly, entirely filling the tunnel.

Joseph Locke gives evidence

The inquest was adjourned for an hour at 5 o'clock and was resumed at 6 o'clock, with Mr. Joseph Locke being sworn in and examined. As the principal engineer of the South Western Railway, he had the general superintendence of the whole line in every department. He has had opportunities of seeing this tunnel during its construction, and it was his duty to approve the works before they are made use of; and he approved Waller's Ash tunnel before the line was opened. At the place

Joseph Locke, 1805–60. Locke was a renowned and respected civil engineer, having worked on several major railway schemes including the Liverpool & Manchester, Grand Junction Railway, Lancaster and Carlisle, Manchester and Sheffield, Caledonian and others.

where the accident happened there was a peculiarity in the construction of this tunnel, as a large conical-shaped piece of chalk fell from the roof of the tunnel after excavation and before the completion of the brickwork, leaving a dome-shaped cavity extending nearly 20 feet above the crown of the arch. It was not a perfect cone, having one side longer than the other. Its width was scarcely so great as the tunnel. The brickwork, in consequence of that slip, was strengthened in that particular place, and from the time the brickwork was built till last Monday no change was observed. In every other part of the tunnel, and of all on the line, the brickwork fits tightly into the solid chalk. In some parts of this tunnel the brickwork springs from the solid chalk; but that is not the case where the accident took place. The brickwork there rises from the bottom. In my opinion the sides of the chalk tunnel are stronger than brickwork. All we have to do is guard against frost and exposure to the weather, which in a tunnel are never severe, and against which proper precautions have been taken by cementing the sides. Some parts have not been cemented, the chalk being left loose, projecting about an inch, with a view of seeing the effect of the weather on it, but no decay whatever has taken place. Wherever this chalk-work has from any cause been found defective, it has in all cases been taken out and brickwork filled in. After the tunnel was completed, a question arose as to the best means of filling up the vacancy above the arch, and it was ultimately determined to sink a

shaft there, which was done, to the depth of about 20 feet, the total depth of the arch being 45 or 50 feet. The arch was perfect. There was no perforation in the brickwork. The entire face of the arch, as far as the cavity extended, was filled up with chalk to a depth of about 10 feet, which was as much as was considered proper to be done, without loading the arch unequally from the irregularities in the shaft. By the subsidence or settlement of the material we calculated that the cavity would be gradually filled up without injuring the brickwork. The shaft was left open; but there was a temporary covering over it. This shaft, unlike all others on the line, was left open, as it was considered probable there might be occasion to add more material at some future time. Nothing more has been done since the partial filling-up of the shaft, which took place when all the other shafts were closed, a few months after the line was opened. His attention was called to this tunnel on Tuesday morning by a guard, at Southampton who reported to him that there was some defect in it. He proceeded by the train to the spot, where he met Mr. Ogilvie, the superintendent under Mr. Brassey, the contractor, and Mr. Martin, the company's superintendent; also Mr. Walker and Mr. Douglas, together with gangers and other persons connected with the works. He learned from Mr. Ogilvie that he had brought Mr. Martin down in consequence of having heard on the previous day some slip had taken place. He went underground, and found there some slipped bricks, which indicated pressure from above, and then went on top where Mr. Martin was, and found a number of men occupied in digging down and widening the shaft, so as to get down to the loose material on the arch. He approved of what they were doing, and ordered them to continue their operations, believing it better to remove the cause rather than attempt to resist it. He afterwards went below and examined the arch more minutely, and with a ladder had an opportunity of testing the arch in every portion. There was only one part, and that to a very small distance on the side of the arch, at all out of shape. It was so small, however, that it was difficult to say whether it had been recently caused, or an unequal settlement after the centres had been taken away. It was scarcely perceptible, and was just above where the 'snipping' of the bricks had taken place. He did not think it necessary to order anything further to be done on that account. The arch in every other respect was of a most perfect form, and there was no brick that had 'snipped' beyond a quarter of an inch in thickness. The 'snipping' was merely the surface, or skin, of the whitewashing peeled off. There was no defect whatever in the materials or construction of the arch. It was the unanimous opinion of all present on the spot, that the fall of earth in the shaft suddenly upon the brickwork had caused the bricks to snip. Although he apprehended no immediate danger, he was convinced that the arch must ultimately be taken out. Locke immediately wrote a letter to Mr. Brassey, calling his attention to all the facts, and he gave orders to Mr. Ogilvie to have men working night and day, in order to relieve the arch. On the following day he was unwell, and did not leave his room, but Mr. Martin reported to him that his orders were being executed and that no change had taken place in the appearance of the arch. That was on Wednesday, and he continued to receive similar reports twice or thrice every day till the accident occurred. He passed through the tunnel on Thursday and Friday last; but did not minutely inspect it. He saw Mr. Brassey on Thursday morning, who told him in consequence of his letter to him, and the reports of his own superintendents, he had sent for his principal miner, Mr. Jones, who was on the Gosport branch, with a view to fix on a plan to take out the arch when the material above had been removed. They determined to erect a stage of timber under the arch. On Friday afternoon he saw part of the timber on the ground for that purpose, and some of the uprights were actually standing in the tunnel. He knew Mr. Jones, as a very superior, practical miner, as good as any in England. On Friday evening Mr. Brassey informed him everything was going on well, though no change had taken place in the arch, which still retained its perfect shape and he was more satisfied with the state of the tunnel that night than before. This was the last report he had. On Saturday morning, the early train not arriving till a late hour, he received from Nine Elms a letter at my chambers in London, telling him of the collapse. He went to Nine Elms station at 1 o'clock and remained there till the next train, which started at 3 o'clock, by which he came down to the spot. Before his departure from Nine Elms, the second and third trains then due, had come in, which told him of the accident in the tunnel. On his arrival, he found that the arch had fallen in immediately under the shaft, to the extent of about 20 feet square, and directly under the apex of the cone to which he had before alluded. The primary cause of the accident was the fall of earth on the arch. He could not account for the sudden giving way of the arch after remaining so long unaltered, except on the supposition that the brickwork having been fractured by the previous fall of chalk, the working of the miners above might have shaken it. The fretting of the arch and snipping of the bricks had rendered it too weak to support the super incumbent mass. If he had seen the brickwork 'snipping' to the extent of one or two barrows-full at a time, even if only to the thickness of one brick, he should certainly have felt alarmed and thought there was danger. If he had been present he would have immediately have had all the men removed; but if after a barrowful had come down the falling had ceased for some hours, as from 4 to 6, and the arch remained perfect, he should have considered it probable that it might have stood for days. He had frequently seen arches that have given way to the extent of one brick thick stand for a long time, but not where there were men working above. He should have considered it safe to work at the top if the arch had been at ease, but if it appeared to be 'fretting' he would have discontinued the working above. He considered Mr. Jones a competent person to form an opinion of the degree of danger that would arise from any change taking place in the state of the arch.

A juror questioned Mr Locke on the thickness of the arch, which was said to vary from 1–18 inches. Where the accident took place the crown of the arch was 2 feet 4 inches and built with cement. The crown had not settled a quarter of an inch. The sides were perfectly solid; and in the whole length of the tunnel there was no deviation from a straight line in the sides of the arch. After he saw the 'snipping' of the bricks, he considered they might have been enabled still to leave the arch without additional support beneath, and he did not believe that any water had penetrated the arch or lodged upon it.

Mr. Bircham, solicitor to the Company, asked about maintenance of the line and Locke stated that the works of the railway are let by contract to Mr. Brassey, under bond. He maintains the rails, the road, the tunnels, and all the work connected with the line, and guarantees their stability. The company has a veto on the appointment of all his officers, so as to ensure efficient and proper superintendence. The line is divided into districts, and the company stipulates that every part of the line shall be examined every day by some one person in every district. We thus maintain a daily surveillance over the whole of the line. It was by this means we obtained, on Monday morning last, a report made to an officer of the company relative to the state of the tunnel, which bought Mr. Martin on the following morning to the spot. The total quantity of earth which fell into the tunnel was from 300 to 400 tons, the whole of which was removed within 36 hours, so that the trains have passed through again this morning.

William Watmore was recalled and asked about the wetness of the material in the tunnel. He noted the chalk taken out of the bottom of the shaft on Wednesday and afterwards was very wet indeed. The weather was wet on Friday; but it was fine on Tuesday, and the chalk taken out on Wednesday was wet.

Thomas Brassey gives evidence

Mr. Thomas Brassey was then sworn in and examined. He lived at Kingston, and was the sole contractor for maintaining the works on the South-Western line. He had been the contractor for that portion of the line in which Waller's Ash tunnel is situated. He corroborated the statement of Mr. Locke, as to the construction of the tunnel, and particularly that portion of it where the fall of chalk originally took place. The shaft was left open, but protected from the weather by a covering of timber and two or three feet of chalk upon it. No wet could find its way into the shaft but what fell perpendicularly. The surface of the ground was drained, so that no water could get down but what fell over the shaft, but whatever soaked through the upper chalk would lodge in the shaft or find its way to the brickwork in the tunnel. There was no change in the tunnel till last Monday. He heard by note received from Mr. Ogilvie, his agent, on Tuesday morning, that there was some 'snipping' of brick seen in the Waller's Ash tunnel, and that Ogilvie would report further in the course of the day. On Tuesday night Ogilvie reported some slight further 'snipping', but that there was no change in the form of the arch, and that he had taken steps to remove the super incumbent weight. That night, Brassey sent a special messenger to Fareham for Thomas Jones and another experienced miner to meet him at the tunnel next morning, that they might devise the best means of proceeding. He also

Thomas Brassey, 1805–1870, was also an engineer but is better known as a contractor. Aside from work in England (*see Rebuilt and the letter by Alan Blackburn),* Brassey was involved in several projects overseas including France and Canada. He is remembered in Winchester as there is a residential road named after him not far from the present railway station.

sent, as a further precaution, to have a large quantity of timber brought to the spot. He went to the tunnel on Wednesday morning, and was there a considerable part of that day and of Thursday and Friday. He examined the tunnel each day carefully, getting up on a ladder and looking at the brickwork, but could not at any time see any change in the form of the arch. On Friday night when he left at 6 o'clock, the snipping was in some places perhaps half a brick deep; in others just a flake off. It was about 20 or 30 feet long on one side at about a quarter of the arch, and about 9 inches wide. No wet had got through the arch, not a drop. The tunnel was whitewashed when completed, but not since, and now is not at all stained by wet. The chalk taken out of the shaft was fine and moist, but not wet. On Thursday and Friday he had a stage of timber (which he had procured from London and Fareham) erected to serve for a scaffold to repair the work at least, or to support the arch if necessary, Mr. Locke having already determined that the damaged part of the arch should be taken out.

On Saturday morning (having gone to Kingston on Friday evening) he was again on his way to the tunnel, when he received intelligence of the accident, and on reaching the spot I found that about eight yards in length of the tunnel had fallen in immediately under the shaft. All the men had been dug out. When the accident happened there were about 12 or 14 feet deep of chalk on this arch; about 10 feet deep had been removed

when he got there. Upon investigating the circumstances, and he did make every enquiry, and could not find that anyone had been to blame for want of due caution or notice of danger. He considered Jones and Hill were as competent a judge of danger as himself had he been there. If he had seen a barrowful of brickwork fall at one time, he should not have apprehended immediate danger either to persons below the part or on it, although it would have shown that the arch was in motion. There would have been more cause for alarm if a second such fall took place, but it is scarcely possible to say, without having seen the falls, how far they threatened danger. It would depend on where and how they fell, which could only be judged by persons seeing them. The labourers had no extra pay for the work over the tunnel, nor any other unusual inducement held out to induce them to undertake it. Watmore (one of the deceased) was a regular sinker, and must himself been a good judge of the extent of danger in such a case. The arch was there three-bricks thick, and set in cement; except at the point where it has fallen, the arch is quite sound to the present time.

Final evidence

Thomas Jones, of Fareham, a miner, had been employed on railways 12 years, and under Mr. Brassey for the last two years. He had never examined Waller's Ash tunnel until last Wednesday morning, when he did so by order of Mr. Brassey. He found the bricks crushed a little on one side, and 'chipping', but not at all displaced, and could not see that its shape was altered in the least. There was no appearance of wet coming through. He did not consider there was any present danger, but by Mr. Brassey's order he proceeded to get a scaffold ready, and to lighten the weight on top of the arch. The work went on day and night, and he saw no difference in the appearance of the arch till Saturday morning, when he arrived at the tunnel at about 20 minutes past six. There had been there a change, succeeded by quiet; about half a barrowful of brickwork had fallen before he got there to a thickness of about 4½ inches. Everything remained quiet till a short time before the accident happened, the men continuing their work above and below. About three or four minutes before the accident a space, 3 or 4 feet square, fell from the top of the arch about 9 inches in thickness. He directly saw danger, and hallooed out to the men to get out of the way, and they had just time to escape when the chalk fell through. He sent no message above; there was no time after I saw the danger to do so. He saw no danger till within two or three minutes before the accident happened, and remained under the shaft myself till the last moment, and never left till all the men were dug out.

John Douglas, of Winchester, was an inspector for Mr. Brassey of the district between Basingstoke and Winchester, and he first received notice from one of his platelayers on Monday morning last of some defect in the Waller's Ash tunnel, which was reported immediately to Mr. Ogilvie. In consequence of this report a number of men were set to work there, and continued without intermission till Friday evening, when he was there till nearly 8 o'clock. He left word with the watchman to give him immediate notice if anything should happen in the night. Up to that time not the slightest change had taken place, but the next morning I was sent for before 6 o'clock. The messenger said that a change had taken place that morning at 4 o'clock in the tunnel for the worse, and that a few more bricks had fallen. He went to the spot immediately, and arrived before 7 o'clock, and found that a barrow full of bricks or pieces of bricks had fallen. He asked Jones what he thought as to danger, and he said he thought no more would come down. Douglas did not at all think it would come in immediately, and continued in the tunnel urging the men on in getting the props in, and then sent a 'signal-man' down the line to signal any engine or train that might be coming to slacken their pace in case anything should happen. Nothing more occurred till about a quarter past seven, when some more bricks fell down, and then the whole almost instantly. Rather before this Jones, being on the scaffolding, had felt something fall on his head, and he then called out that we should send to make sure no one was in the shaft, and instantly despatched a man for that purpose. Someone at the time observed that word had been sent up. The man Douglas spoke to went, but it was not above a minute after that the tunnel fell in, those in it having barely time to escape by running backwards before the whole mass came in.

George Price was recalled, to be asked about his dealings with Ferris. When Ferris came to work with his men at 6 o'clock on Saturday morning, Price told him he had taken off his men at 4 o'clock that morning because he thought there was danger. He wished Ferris to look at the brickwork, which he did, and he said he thought there was no danger. There had been a second fall very shortly after the first, and when Ferris came there must have been five or six barrow loads fallen in all. When Ferris said he thought there was no danger, Price did not contradict him, but was still of the same opinion as before, and should not, if it had been his turn to come on with his men at six, have allowed them to go into the hole unless some of the gentlemen, such as Mr. Locke or Mr. Martin, had seen it.

William Capon, of Fareham, superintendent over labourers for Mr. Brassey, had come to the work at Waller's Ash tunnel last Friday with a gang of men. No change took place during Friday. He got to the tunnel at half past 6 o'clock Saturday morning, and found Ferris at the top, but did not go down into the tunnel that morning until after the accident. Ferris told him a few bricks had fallen from the arch. The men were all at work when he got there, some in the tunnel and some in the shaft. He was on the top and had no notice from below until after the accident happened. Ferris had no conversation that morning as to any increased danger. Ferris was two minutes before the accident standing on the upper stage in the shaft, and if he had remained two minutes longer, would have perished more likely than almost any man.

The jury's verdict

The coroner checked with the jury whether they wished to hear any more evidence and as they did not he proceeded to sum up. The main object of the inquiry, to ascertain the immediate cause of death of these unfortunate men, he thought that the

facts which had been proved should undoubtedly lead them to return a verdict of accidental death. The other question which arose incidentally but unavoidably out of the former – namely, to investigate the cause of the accident as between the Railway Company and the public – i.e. whether it arose from any degree of carelessness on their part, and whether any precautions by way of notice to the workmen in the shaft could have prevented it. They had heard the whole circumstances described from the original formation of the tunnel up to the time this unhappy occurrence took place. The tunnel had been erected and placed under the inspection of the most able officers; and nothing wrong having occurred for two years there was perhaps no reasonable expectation of an accident. Notice of the 'snipping' of the brickwork in the arch was taken on Monday last, and everything had been done that could be done up till Saturday morning. The question was, whether more might not have been done. The employment in the shaft seemed to have been unpleasant, the men objecting to go into it, not so much from apprehension of danger as on account of the inconvenience. Price, one of the foremen, noticed a change at 4 o'clock that morning, some of the brickwork having fallen in, which induced him to remove his men from their employment within the tunnel. Indications of danger seemed to have increased up to the time Ferris reached the spot, two hours afterwards. Price communicated his apprehensions to Ferris, and showed him about six barrows full of bricks that had fallen – whole bricks continuing to fall. Now this fact that whole bricks continued to fall, showed that there must have been a considerable loosening of that part of the arch, therefore there was some cause for the apprehension existing in Price's mind. Ferris however, did not appear to have seen the danger in the same light, while Jones did not apprehend any danger until almost immediately before the accident occurred. But these were all merely subordinate officers, and the work was left to the superintendence of illiterate men, Jones, for instance could not write his name. He really did think that persons of that uneducated class should not have been left in charge of so dangerous portion of the line. Some more competent officer than Ferris should have been present on the occasion, who, on finding the fall of brickwork to increase so greatly between 4 and 6 o'clock, would at once have seen the propriety of at all events removing the men who were at work within the shaft, and under the tunnel. To use the expression of Price, someone of the 'Gentlemen' officers should have been present for that purpose. That was the only point in which blame could be attached to the company, who were ultimately responsible for all the acts of those employed under them. How far they were blameworthy in that respect he would leave the jury to pronounce. There could be no doubt the materials which fell in on this occasion, having once separated from the freehold, were as soon as the accident had occurred subject to the law of deodand,[1] and only redeemable on payment of such a sum as the verdict of a jury might award. Deodands were regulated invariably by the circumstances of the case and the degree of blame attached to the parties. Sometimes they were merely nominal, and in the case of a recent railway accident the deodand imposed was no less than

£1,000. The jury must consider themselves arbitrators between the public and the railway company, giving them credit so far as they had done their best, but still holding a tight rein over those parties at whose mercy we were all more or less placed, under the present mode of travelling. He must leave it to them, avoiding extremes, to assess what amount they thought proper as a deodand. If they thought no blame attached either to the company or to their servants, they would be perfectly justified in making it nominal; if otherwise, they might give any sum between 1s. and the full value of the goods forfeited. He now called upon them to consider their verdict.

The jury retired at a quarter to 11 o'clock, and after an absence of 35 minutes the following verdict was delivered: 'Accidental death in each case, with a deodand of £50 on the materials that fell. The jury consider that Henry Ferris, the foreman of the deceased, was not a fit and competent person to be entrusted with the lives of men in so important a work.' The Coroner said he entirely concurred in the verdict, and he had great pleasure in being enabled to say this, instead of being compelled to declare that he took it as their finding and not his. The proceeding did not finish till midnight.

The government inspector

Wallers Ash was not the only tunnel giving the LSWR some concerns. At Fareham on the Gosport branch there had already been a major collapse, and the Government Inspector, Major-General Pasley, was visiting the site from time to time. Thus it was convenient for him to stop off at Wallers Ash tunnel on his way to Fareham and inspect the site of the accident. He visits first on Wednesday, 6 April but his report does not appear to have survived.

On 13 April he again visits and reports back to the President of the Board of Trade:

In my report of Wednesday 6 April upon the accident, after having inspected the work then in progress for repairing the broken part of the arch of the Tunnel and securing the chalk above, I stated my opinion that everything was going on well, and that if rightly informed as to the thickness of the brickwork and the state of the chalk above in other parts of the tunnel and in the three tunnels near it, of which points it is obviously impossible to judge by inspection of the work when finished, I had no hesitation in saying that all three tunnels were in a safe state. Notwithstanding this impression, on Tuesday last, six days after my first inspection, I took the opportunity of examining work at Wallers Ash Tunnel a second time on my return from Gosport, and I found that good progress had been made, the breach in the arch of the tunnel having been substantially repaired with brickwork laid in cement, and entirely chased with the exception of a manhole by which the workmen ascend and get up their materials. Labourers were then employed in spreading and ramming loose chalk over the brickwork of the tunnel preparatory to sloping off the sides of the open chamber in the chalk above it.

Yesterday, Mr Martin, the resident engineer, at whose request partly I made this second inspection, took me into a gallery in the chalk which I had not seen before, as the mouth of it was then closed and which had not been described to me. It is about 30 feet long, 15 or 16 feet wide and 7½ feet high in the form of a natural arch, in the same direction with and immediately over the Tunnel to the northward of the part that fell in recently, with which it communicated. This gallery appeared to be composed of sound chalk, and had been formed by the first downfall of that material, which crushed this portion of the Tunnel, before the railway was opened as mentioned in my former letter. At that period after having repaired the arch beneath it, instead of filling up the hole, they left it open, but took the precaution of supporting it by rough woodwork, consisting of 4 transverse frames with longitudinal timber over and on each side of them. This arrangement no doubt must have prevented the chalk above the gallery from falling and crushing the portion of tunnel beneath it. On the 2 April when the recent accident occurred, Mr Martin informed me that he had instructions to build some arch ribs of brickwork laid in cement, to replace the woodwork, which may be expected to decay in a few years, and that it was also in contemplation to fill up this gallery in order to ensure its permanent security. My opinion is that when no vacant spaces are left above the brickwork of a Tunnel, in the sort of chalk near Winchester, it may be considered safe; and that the filling up of the gallery with chalk rubbish carefully rammed may suffice, though the additional brickwork will no doubt be beneficial. After examining this gallery I went up to the top, where I observed some cracks in the chalk above the spot where the men were at work, which was at the bottom of the chasm formed by the last accident, about 45 feet below the surface. Not having noticed these cracks when I visited the same spot before, I pointed them out to Mr Martin and suggested, that if the chalk below were injudiciously moved when levelling it, a second accident similar to the former might take place, which might be prevented by him or his assistant Engineer being constantly on the spot, instead of leaving the execution of the work to common labourers and a Foreman. Agreeing with me in opinion, he directed that the practice of working by night, when the state of the chalk could not be seen in so deep a hole should be discontinued. Thus the matter rests. Neglect or want of judgement may occasion an accident, but I apprehend none and should have no objection to remain on the spot myself, where the men are at work, provided that they are properly superintended. I wrote to Mr Locke the Engineer in Chief to state my apprehension and to recommend him to examine the spot again.

I beg to add that there is an immense mound of spoil or refuse chalk upon the surface piled immediately over the portion of the gallery described in this letter, and on the very brink of the chamber produced by the last accident. This is an additional reason for anxiety and precaution. But under ordinary circumstances, I should not think it reasonable to require any person of more skill or importance than a Foreman to superintend the removal of chalk, nor would I have suggested such a thing if I had not observed the suspicious cracks before alluded to.

Resumption of traffic through the tunnel

The line reopened for traffic on Monday, 4 April, and that night the newspapers were able to report another accident close to the tunnel, this time happily with no serious consequences. An engine, going up to Nine Elms to be repaired, with the 8 o'clock

This time it is a 'King Arthur' that is seen, and on the up line shortly to enter Wallers Ash tunnel. The date is 20 February 1960 and the engine No. 30768 *Sir Balin*.

luggage train, ran off the line, dragging with it the tender, and became embedded in the earth. Some alarm was manifested in case the mail train should arrive, and run into the luggage train, as the down line was blocked by the scaffolding erected in the tunnel. It was impossible to extricate the stricken engine, but after considerable exertions, the train was taken to Winchester, where it crossed on to the down line, and on passing the engine in the cutting, recrossed, by means of extra points, on to the up line, reaching Vauxhall station nearly two hours late.

A subsequent newspaper report reassured the public that an accident between the mail train and the luggage train was impossible, as there were three intervening watchmen, who would have given notice of the trouble. These reports suggest that single-line working had been instituted through the tunnel, with extra points being installed. Presumably, to erect staging under the fallen arch, the up line would have been slewed over at this point.

On Saturday night when the accident was known about at Nine Elms station, it was thought that passengers would transfer to the 'Red Rover' stagecoach that was still running between London and Southampton but instead of being full the coach contained one passenger.

Modern-day conclusions

Some accident reports from earliest days can be dry to read and seemingly of little relevance to present-day conditions. Not so this one and we should, of course, remember that it was in consequence of incidents that safety standards were devised resulting in the modern-day rule book commensurate with safe working.

There are also several interesting points raised – and even missed in the report – which are worthy of brief investigation. Firstly we learn there were three other tunnels: two immediately north of Micheldever and that at Litchfield summit, the point here being that we now have confirmation that the two Micheldever tunnels were always that – two separate tunnels – and not as has been suggested a single tunnel later opened out in the centre to form a deep cutting.

We also have mention of a guard having experienced something wrong/falling as his train passed through. It is perhaps surprising this man was not either questioned by the engineer's or even called to the inquest. Hence we have no idea as to what he might have experienced.

Reading through we might also express surprise that it appeared, and indeed was confirmed towards the end of the report, that trains were permitted to continue passing through when scaffolding was in place. The immediate conclusion was that there was only a single line in place – temporarily – but it appears two sets of rails were present but with one only in use at the time.

Then we have mention of a 'signal-man' whilst later the term 'watchman' is used. In fact there is mention of three watchmen in the vicinity. A 'signal-man' at the time was literally just that at this period, 'a man who signalled to the trains' no doubt with a flag, arm signal, or perhaps even a board. Finally, we have mention of a 'miner' working on the Gosport branch. This should not be taken literally as meaning 'being at Gosport' as there were never any tunnels there, but instead contemporaneously the 'Gosport branch' was referred to as starting at Eastleigh and no doubt the miners were engaged in the tunnels around Fareham. Here remember additional lines of bricks had to be set on to the inside of the tunnel rendering it no longer wide enough for two sets of rails and consequently just a single line has persisted ever since. It is fortunate the same option was not undertaken at Wallers Ash but the strata through which each tunnel passes was very different in both places.

Obviously there are no images or even engravings of the incident or remedial work from the 1840s but the reader is directed to the following websites that both depict the south portal where the collapse occurred, and give a good indication of the depth of the cutting and what a long way it was between those working in the tunnel and those on top.

http://svsfilm.com/nineelms/bassett.htm

www.prorail.co.uk/BWselection.php?id=225

---

[1] A deodand is a thing forfeited or given to God, specifically, in law, an object or instrument that becomes forfeited because it has caused a person's death. The English common law of deodands traces back to the eleventh century and was applied, on and off, until Parliament finally abolished it in 1846. (Wikipedia) Possibly the other deodand referred to, of £1,000, referred to the accident on the GWR in Sonning Cutting on Christmas Eve, 1841 – some three-and-a-half months before the Waller's Ash accident, as a result of which the Coroner's jury put a deodand of £1,100 on the locomotive *Hecla* and the wagons of her train – there is a Wikipedia entry that describes it, and it is also in Hamilton Ellis's *Four Main Lines*, and in MacDermott, to give but two references. In that case the deodand was later overturned, and never paid. It would be interesting to know if this one was paid, since Hamilton Ellis implied that deodands were abolished after the Sonning accident (although clearly the law hadn't been changed by April 1842).

Field Trip to Margate Sands

Alan Postlethwaite

One Sunday in April 1959, starting at the crack of dawn, a friend and I bought cheap day return tickets at Victoria for a pilgrimage to the Isle of Thanet. Our mission was to photograph the last vestiges of steam on the LC&DR. Having duly recorded 'Pacifics', 'Moguls' and 'Schools' between Faversham and Margate, we could not also resist taking a quick look at Margate Sands station. This was once the terminus of the SER main line branch from Ramsgate Town. It closed in 1926 when Thanet was rationalised. Exploring further up the trackbed, we discovered sidings to the south of the BR main line with old coaching stock in store. In the end we walked the entire SER branch to Ramsgate, a long stretch of which was spanned by gantries carrying electricity cables with the unadopted footpath below. Along the way there was a level crossing with great concrete blocks to impede the Wehrmacht in the event of invasion. There was also a cavern dug into a chalk cutting that turned out to be an old air raid shelter.

The SR's Continental stock had straight narrow sides with guard's windows at the ends. The storage sidings joined the BR main line to the east of Margate station. They extended about half a mile inland, slowly being swallowed by the brambles and track weed. 'Come in, Number 696!'

Here is the sumptuous interior of one of the stored coaches – an open second of Continental stock. Built by the SR in 1931 to an SE&CR design, this was originally a general saloon or nondescript, one of three saloons that could be designated first, second or third class according to traffic needs. They were used on boat trains to Dover, Folkestone and Gravesend, Britain's very last second class services. *All five illustrations are by the author and are copyright of the Bluebell Railway Photographic Archive*

Margate Sands station had a prime location on the seafront. What a wonderful frontage, like nothing else on the SER! Its new uses were in the spirit of the Jolly Boys Outing in the *Fools and Horses* TV sitcom. One can imagine too the thrill of Victorians arriving here, perhaps to enjoy the seaside for the first time in their lives. The adjacent cinema, in brick, was once the site of an LC&DR terminus to handle local traffic to Ramsgate but it was never used, becoming a dance hall instead. All LC&DR traffic used the new (1863) through station, which the SR rebuilt in 1926. Margate Sands closed in 1926, Ramsgate Town station had already closed during the First World War, having been badly damaged in a Zeppelin raid. Dreamland fun fair originated in 1880: it was rejuvenated in the 1920s and again in 2015. The one thing that we forgot on that day was to visit the beach!

Margate Sands engine shed had become a warehouse with all windows and vents blanked off. The brickwork looks nearly new.

A view from the Margate Sands branch across Ramsgate allotment gardens. Two trains are passing on the 1926 cut-off that connected the LC&DR and SER main lines. The steam train is on its way to Margate and possibly Victoria. The Hastings DEMU is a mystery, possibly a Sunday Excursion Special. Our long day ended with a quick visit to the former LC&DR terminus at Ramsgate Harbour. Only the tunnel remained, carrying a narrow gauge railway. The station area had been completely overbuilt for leisure and amusement. Anyone for a pint of whelks?

We arrived home after dark, tired and hungry. I had carried a sandwich box and an army water bottle in my duffle bag together with a tripod and cycle cape. The whole trip had cost each of us 70p in rail tickets and for me about 50p for film and developing – wonderful value for an enjoyable day of railway exploration. Even so, I could not afford to print all thirty-nine photos, nor did I have access to a darkroom, hence they remained unseen for some thirty-five years. My entire negative collection has since been scanned by the Bluebell Railway Archives team and is available on their website.

Motorman of 1909

From the Southern Region Magazine of 1959 *(yes 'Southern Region'!)*

The Regional Editor meets a Motorman of 1909

Are you old enough to remember the LB & SCR overhead electric trains that ran between Victoria and London Bridge, to the Crystal Palace, and in later years, to Coulsdon North? Those smart trains, operated on 6,600 volts AC, but had to give way eventually to the Southern's standard third-rail 660 volts DC system, and the last 'overhead' electric service actually ran from Victoria to Coulsdon North on the night of 21 September 1929. This being the golden jubilee year of the Brighton 'elevated electrics', as they were called – the South London line from Victoria to London Bridge was electrified in December 1909 – I went down to Edenbridge to see, by invitation, Mr Charles McAuliffe, who was one of the pioneer motormen of those trains (he retired in 1947 as a driving inspector). Living in a charming bungalow in the country, I found Mr McAuliffe hale and hearty, for all his 72 years.

Electric bogie power van used when the service was extended to Coulsdon North and Sutton. These would normally work sandwiched between a pair of trailers on either side with the complete train being driven from the front or rear – as required. As 'locomotives', and so able to be driven independently, they could also be used to haul an ordinary train but we do not know if this ever took place. No. 10101 is seen at the builders, the Metropolitan Carriage & Wagon Finance Co., at Saltley – better known later as 'Metropolitan Cammell'. As is known these vehicles were, after the demise of the 'overhead', converted into the first series of bogie-brake vans.

History

'The history of those trains,' said Mr McAuliffe, 'is unknown to most people to-day. The LB & SCR company, alarmed at the loss of traffic through the electrification of the London trams, which took place in 1904, decided to electrify their suburban lines, and made a start on the South London line. The work was given to a German firm who made a remarkably good job of all the overhead equipment.

'The motormen's jobs were offered to engine drivers, but few were interested, so guards were then given the opportunity of becoming motormen. I was a guard at the time – I joined the service in 1903 – so I became a motorman.' The directors of the company, said Mr McAuliffe, preferred the overhead wire to the third rail as the former was becoming increasingly popular on the Continent for long-distance work and the LB & SCR board had in mind the future electrification of their main line to Brighton. This idea materialised many years later, when the Southern Railway electrified this line but on the third-rail principle in 1933. Contact with the overhead wire was made by means of bows fitted to the roofs of the motor coaches. The bows lay flat on the roofs when the train was not in use. Mr McAuliffe explained that to raise the bows you had to work by hand an air pump, but once contact was established the current kept them up.

The South London line was such a success that the Victoria–Crystal Palace line was electrified in 1911, and the London Bridge–Tulse Hill line in the following year.

Flash-back to 1911 when Mr McAuliffe drove trains on those lines. He recalls the great Festival of Empire at the Crystal Palace in 1911, to commemorate the coronation of King George V and Queen Mary. This was the biggest exhibition of its time and brought thousands of visitors to 'The Palace'. The railway ran many special trains and traffic was heavy. In those days, he said, we motormen worked a 10-hour day. It was not until 1919 that we got the eight-hour day. In 1925 the lines to Wallington and Coulsdon North were electrified. The Southern Railway had then been in existence two years as a result of the amalgamation of 1923, but this work had been started by the Brighton company. For these lines powerful electric locomotives were used, positioned in the middle of the train. The motorman drove from a driving trailer at either end. Although as a driving inspector in later years, Mr McAuliffe had many important trips on the Brighton main line – he was usually in the driver's cab when royalty were travelling – he says he was happiest in the old days. All the LB & SCR motormen and guards had smart uniforms with silver buttons which had to be polished regularly. The overhead electric trains ran very smoothly; it was a pleasure to drive them. Nowadays Mr McAuliffe, who is a great-grandfather, spends his time in gardening, house decorating, and meeting at regular intervals some of his old colleagues. And there are many old friends still working on the Southern to whom he sends his kind regards.

Forest Fires

SOUTHERN RAILWAY.

CIRCULAR NO. 56.

GENERAL MANAGER'S OFFICE,
WATERLOO STATION,
LONDON, S.E.1.
31st May, 1927.

RAILWAY FIRES ACTS, 1905 & 1923.

DAMAGE TO FORESTS, PLANTATIONS, WOODS, ORCHARDS, MARKET AND NURSERY GARDENS, AGRICULTURAL LAND, CROPS AND MEADOW LAND BY FIRE.

Jeffery Grayer recalls a Southern Railway Circular of 1927 highlighting forested lineside areas at risk from passing locos:

Lineside fires are a problem still with us today even though steam locomotives have disappeared from regular use for more than fifty years. The occasional 'steam bans' affecting the operation of preserved steam locomotives over the national network are still invoked, particularly during times of exceptionally dry weather, whilst some of the heritage lines have had their own issues on occasions. Modern track maintenance involving the use of grinding and welding machines, which can give off sparks, may also set fire to tinder-dry vegetation, especially as lineside growth is far less well controlled today than in times past.

Back in 1927, the SR obviously thought the problem needed highlighting in one of their periodic circulars issued from time to time. Circular No. 56 of 31 May 1927 drew the attention of various grades of staff to the need to be vigilant. Gangers, locomotive drivers and firemen and shed staff were all singled out for special instructions, the main thrust of which was to be alert to the dangers of

Above and opposite top: **Alice Holt Forest near Bentley station on the Alton line. The line branching off at Bentley is the former Bordon branch closed to passengers in 1957.**
Wokingham Forest lies between Wokingham station and Wellington College station which was renamed Crowthorne in 1928.

starting conflagrations, to reduce the likelihood of fires breaking out and if they had to extinguish them, to do so promptly. In this regard, gangers were tasked to undertake regular inspections of areas of the line that adjoined forested areas. They were instructed to cut down any undergrowth that might easily be set alight by sparks and to dispose of such vegetation by burning – providing this could be done safely – or by clearing the cuttings away. Where forested areas adjoined the line, gangers were requested to approach the landowners with a view to having any undergrowth likely to be a fire hazard on private land cut away. Should the landowner refuse then gangers had the right to enter upon the land and undertake the cutting themselves providing that they did not cause any damage to trees, bushes or shrubs. The prior agreement of the Divisional or District Engineer must be sought in such cases. Locomotive crews were instructed to exercise caution when traversing such forested areas especially during exceptionally dry weather, ensuring that they did not drive or fire in such a manner as to cause the undue emission of sparks.

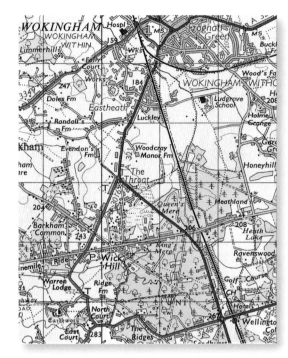

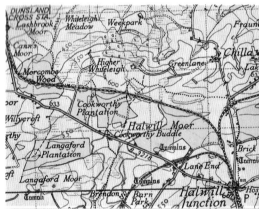

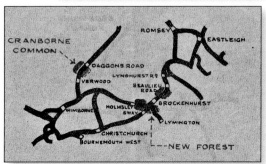

Top left and below: **Halwill Forest showing the forested areas adjacent to the Halwill–Bude line between Dunsland Cross and Halwill Junction stations.**

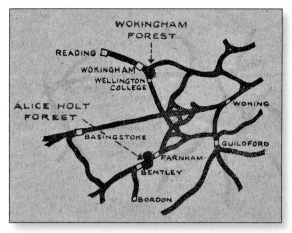

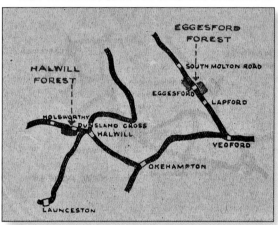

Centre left and above: **Eggesford Forest in the vicinity of Eggesford station on the Exeter–Barnstaple line.**

Left, below left and below: **The New Forest, especially in the vicinity of Holmsley station on the Brockenhurst–Ringwood line. Bedgebury Forest, shows the forested area adjacent to the Hawkhurst branch line between Goudhurst and Cranbrook stations.**

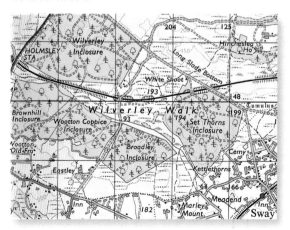

They were also instructed not to throw hot ashes from moving locomotives. Shed staff were encouraged to keep baffle plates and brick arches on locomotives in good condition, whilst all staff were instructed to keep a sharp lookout on the lineside or adjoining land whilst undertaking their duties.

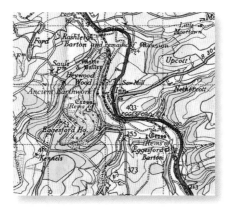

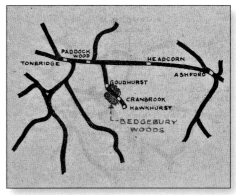

There followed instructions on the 'Detection and Extinguishing of fires on the lineside' aimed at enginemen, permanent way staff, signalmen and crossing keepers, stationmasters, permanent way inspectors and gangers. When enginemen spotted a fire they were

Above: **Cranborne Common adjacent to the Salisbury–West Moors line in the vicinity of Daggons Road station.**

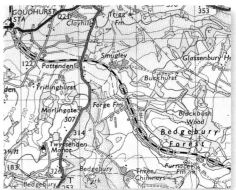

told to give one crow followed by one long and one crow whistle and to repeat this procedure when passing the next signal box, permanent way man or station. Upon hearing these whistles the signalman, crossing keeper or other staff should arrange for the stationmaster or permanent way man nearest the outbreak to be advised promptly. On being advised of a fire, the PW man should proceed with all speed to the location with all available staff. The stationmaster had the responsibility of ensuring that any fire was effectively attended to by the Engineering Department or, if he was unable to do so, that he proceeded with all available staff to the site of the incident. There was, of course, a form for reporting such fires to the Head of Department for the area concerned. There was naturally no obligation to request prior permission to enter land at the site of the fire, although it was stated that as a matter of courtesy landowners should be informed after the event, although of course this might prompt a claim! The instruction was signed by Herbert Walker, the General Manager of the SR.

These instructions reflected the fact that under the Railway Fires Acts of 1905 and 1923 the railway was liable for damage to forests, woods, plantations, orchards, market and nursery gardens, agricultural land or fences and any crops thereon resulting from sparks emitted by locomotives, and such claims could prove costly. The following diagrams specified in red some of the significant areas most at risk but the attention of staff was drawn to the fact that all points of contact between forested areas and railway lines were possible sources of danger. Sections from later OS maps have been appended alongside some of these designated high-risk areas to show the areas of risk in more detail.

Many of these areas highlighted no longer enjoy the luxury of a train service. The Hawkhurst branch closed in 1961, the Bude branch in 1966 and the Salisbury–West Moors line, together with the 'Old Road' through Holmsley from Brockenhurst to Wimborne, closed in 1964. Electric and diesel traction have, of course, reduced fire risks since steam days, however, as previously mentioned, even today lineside fires can be a major headache for the rail industry with these

starting for a number of reasons, such as discarded cigarettes and matches, arson attempts, and electrical faults. Smoke also reduces visibility, while cable fires can damage signalling equipment and associated cabling, not to mention property, along the track, all of which severely disrupts train services.

To prevent lineside fires the rail industry is continually evolving a long-term vegetation management plan to reduce the risks.

During hot weather litter clearance programmes are arranged and staff proactively report on any build-up of rubbish along the tracks. Track workers are equipped with fire extinguishers when they undertake 'hot work' such as welding. It is ensured that grinding trains, which generate a lot of sparks when they reshape worn rails, have ample water on board and operators have had training about fire risks.

(The Editor has his own memories of travelling by train through the New Forest in the early 1960s and seeing stands of Fire Beaters at intervals alongside the line. Folklore has it that the occasional unscrupulous arable farmer might even deliberately set his field alight to claim compensation, especially perhaps if it was a poor crop.)

(Extracts from OS maps, all pre-1960, courtesy of the Controller of the Ordnance Survey)

So how do lineside fires occur? Clearly due to any one (or more) of several reasons, some are given in the main text and others as simple as a discarded cigarette or a sliver of hot metal from a brake block. So far as the locomotive is concerned, there are again many reasons; an unexpected slip perhaps throwing cinders high into the air, poor coal or even an over-enthusiastic fireman – or driver. Dropped cinders from the ash pan might be another cause. In this case though all appears to be well. No. 34005 *Barnstaple* immediately south of Shawford on 12 September 1965 with the Sunday 08.53 Bournemouth to Waterloo and another excellent view from *Tony Molyneaux*

EMU Recognition Part 2
The LB&SCR Elevated Electrics
Richard Whitbread

The LB&SCR were early adopters of electric power for their lines, with authorisation for using such power being included in their parliamentary Act of 1903. The view of the LB&SCR management was that electrification made economic and technical sense – lower running costs as well as a need to counter falling traffic on the South London line, which then ran from Victoria to London Bridge at high level – hence their naming as the 'Elevated Electrics'. Overhead electrification was seen as more appropriate for long-distance travel to the coast.

The rolling stock for this initial scheme (public service commenced on 1 December 1909, some six months later than the original plan due to delays in meeting external requirements) was formed in three car units. The LB&SCR decided on purpose-built rolling stock and eight units each of three coaches were ordered from the Metropolitan Amalgamated Carriage and Wagon Company and constructed at Saltley. The stock was designed by Philip Dawson and D.E. Marsh, the locomotive superintendent, although Albert Panter was also responsible as the line's carriage and wagon foreman but fine details may have been left to the manufacturer.

The design of the stock took advantage of the generous loading gauge available on the line and measurements were to a common standard across the coaches. The two vehicle types – Driving Motor Brake Third (DMBT) and Trailer First (TF) – had common measurements: 60ft long by 9ft wide over body panels, 63ft 7in long over buffers by 9ft 5in wide over handles, but 9ft 1in wide at the cantrail. They were 12ft 3in high. There is some suggestion that the width permitted sliding door stock which was being introduced on contemporary electrified lines but it seems likely the winning tender with compartments was cheaper. The coaches were connected with screw couplings and standard buffers. Bogie centres were at 41ft 0in and all bogies were of 8ft 0in wheelbase with pressed steel frames, wheel diameter was 3ft 7½in.

Much thought was given to safety. The coaches were constructed on steel plate underframes (these had quite deep

South London Line stock, October 1908. DBMT No. 3203 leads, with TF No. 3202 as the centre vehicle. Of note is the conventional strong underframe and 'LV' (last vehicle) flag. At this stage in history, and notwithstanding the quiet approach these trains would have made, the LBSCR, like its successor the SR and then BRS, did not consider the need to make the front end more visible to staff working on the line.

strengthening girders between the bogies, giving these units (and other subsequent 'AC' design units) a distinctive appearance) with timber bodies that were covered in sheet aluminium at the sides (12swg), ends (12swg) and over the roof (21swg). The reason for the sheet aluminium was to enable any electric currents to be transmitted to earth if an overhead cable should break and fall on a train. To prevent damage from a broken (or sagging) conductor wire, external wooden transverse ribs were provided to the arc profile roofs, which had no vents (there were instead vents above each door). There were double floors filled with slag wool over Uralite insulating material and aluminium sheeting that was again earthed by connection to the underframe. Since cables ran through the floors, steel could not be used as secondary currents might have been induced that would have had the effect of providing unwanted additional heat. The stock was solidly built and typically saw service for forty-five years.

At the outer end, each unit had a motor coach with a driver's compartment accessed from the guard/luggage compartment. The two were separated by a conventional door but there was also a circular door so that either driver or guard could access the handbrake. The roof of the motor coach dropped down above the driver and guard compartments to provide space for the two collector bows of a unique design prepared by Dawson. The rear bow, in relation to the direction of travel of each pair, was raised on both motor coaches (bows can only trail, unlike pantographs) as there were no power line connections between the two motor coaches and there was an interconnection that ensured only matching pairs of bows could be raised. The bows were 5ft 2in wide and the collecting strips, made of aluminium, were 3ft 7¼in wide. The collector strips had a life of 5,000 to 6,000 miles (four to five weeks in normal service). The equipment mounted on the roof was all 'live' when either bow was raised and it was therefore surrounded by a protective basket that was installed sometime after the units were delivered. As evidence exists of the units without the basket; it is believed these were installed prior to service commencing. *(Does this perhaps even indicate there had been safety issues – Ed?)*

Compressed air was used to raise the bows with changeover at termini; the second bow being raised before the first was lowered. When on a depot and off power, the bows could be raised using a small hand pump carried on each train. Originally the bows had a second collector, which was sprung against the conductor wire, but it was found that these were unnecessary to ensure continuous power and were soon removed.

South London line train, 6 November 1908. Again we see DMBT No. 3203 is in the lead. Evidently oil headlamps were also in use. Note too the wording of the air pipes 'Train' and 'Bow', the latter the contemporary term for the roof pantograph. The stock was then brand new; hence the white tyres.

The motor coaches were each equipped with 115hp[1] single-phase AC motors – four in number, one driving each axle. These motors were the most powerful then available and patented by Winter Eichberg but constructed by AEG in Berlin. Each motor coach carried two 220kW mains transformers, mounted on the underframes, which turned the supply (6,700v) into traction power at a maximum 750V with contactors, which enabled power initially at 450v, then 580v, then 640v and finally 750 volts (as it was increased through contactors) to reach the motors. One transformer supplied each pair of motors. A further transformer provided power for the other electrical circuits – the control system, the Westinghouse brake compressor and the carriage lighting – all at 300V. Only the lower voltage was passed along the trailer coaches. The compressor maintained the air reservoir pressure at 110lb per in² and the train air pipe was regulated at 70lb per in². There was a compressor on each motor and these were powered by a 6hp two-pole motor, which supplied air for both the brakes and for raising the bow collectors.

The electrical equipment (comprising high-tension switches, fuses and auxiliary transformer) were in fireproof cabinets accessed through doors in the guard's compartment and were mounted right at the front of the coach adjacent to the driver's compartment. Opening the doors of the cabinets ensured that the collector bow was lowered and disconnected and also earthed the electrical equipment. One source quotes the gear ratio was 4.24 to 1, but Brown refers to 25:83, which is 3.23 to 1. Equipment in the cab included meters showing voltage, amperage and wattage plus a brake pressure gauge. The master controller incorporated a simple 'deadman' device requiring constant pressure by the driver – if the pressure was released the current was disconnected and the brakes were applied.

Externally the coaches were painted with umber brown lower panels and cream upper panels. Under the window of each door the class was indicated with the inward one of the two guard's compartment doors showing 'GUARD'. Various panels at the same height were either blank, showed the coach number or the initials 'LB&SCR'. Each door plus side windows to driver and equipment compartment had ventilators.

The 300V power cables ran the entire length of the cars, providing lighting and control signals. Two multiple unit jumpers were positioned below the headstocks and located below the panel line running down the inside of the driver's window and panelled window in front of the equipment compartment. There were loose jumper cables to enable connection. At the driving coach ends there were two connecting hoses; one for the Westinghouse air brakes and the other for the bow collector air pipe. Between vehicles in the set there was a main reservoir-equalising pipe connection.

Initial seating capacities were recorded as: DMBT thirty-three smoking, thirty-three non-smoking; TF twenty-five

smoking, thirty-one non-smoking. Total capacity, 188. There was no second-class accommodation as the LB&SCR felt that there was no need for an intermediate class – with the third class generally being similar to previous second class – and consequently the LB&SCR were the first to omit second class. Subsequent reports show a higher seating capacity with the generous width in third class enabling them to seat five a side (six at each end of the coach) to give forty-one smoking and forty-one non-smoking, eighty-two in total. (Moody, for some reason, records seventy-two). As the first-class coaches were fitted with arm rests it is hard to see how these could be reported as seventy-four (Moody again).

The motor coaches contained eight 'compartments' each of 6ft width and weighing 54 tons. The first class coach comprised nine 'compartments' each of 6ft 6in width and weighing 32 tons. In both cases there was a corridor that swapped sides at the midpoint to equalise the weight distribution and also divided the coach into smoking and non-smoking seats. Internally, the rolling stock was well fitted, each compartment having two carbon filament electric lamps (which had a very rapid flicker), the third class being upholstered to a high standard and more spacious than other suburban stock. Despite the gangways, there was a door on each side of the coach providing access to each compartment. It was noted that this permitted rapid ingress and egress of passengers to shorten station stops. Although the corridor was not perpetuated on later stock, the application of a door to each 'compartment' on suburban stock was followed with little exception until the introduction of class 508s. The word compartment is deliberately in inverted commas, as there was nothing between the seating bays apart from double luggage racks (umbrella rack below a larger rack) or at the end of the seating row to the gangway – so it was very much 'open' as would be seen in '4-VEP' units.

The first class was upholstered with a brown tapestry (Gould mentions blue) and folding intermediate armrests. Third class was red and black repp material (a cloth woven in fine cords). There were ornate panels attached as an arch over the side corridors between bodyside and the divider between the seats.

Each bay had a door on both sides, doors having the usual droplight within and having a quarter-light window on each side. Above each quarter-light window a further much smaller rectangular window was provided. These could be partly opened by hinging outwards from one end. A fluted air ventilator with the vent along the bottom edge was provided above each door droplight, while there were other similar ones in the luggage van doors, above the driver's droplight and one in the bodyside between the luggage doors and the first passenger quarter-light. At some point post-delivery the door droplights for the smoking areas had the word SMOKING etched into the glass. Also, the motor coach door drop lights had three window bars added horizontally to prevent passengers putting their heads out.

From within the motorman's cab there was a control that permitted the display of either a white light (known as a 'head disk') or a tail disk (a red light) as appropriate. This was modified when the units were re-formed as it no longer stretched across

---

[1] A number of resources, including Brown, quote a power of 120hp. Brown qualifies this as a one-hour rating, the others do not. It is also worth noting that Howard-Turner specifically says that when re-formed the motors were changed to the 150hp standard used on later stock, I have not seen mention of this elsewhere.

Interior of the guard's/motorman's compartment of the South London stock. The cubicle doors to the high-tension cupboards are open. A conventional and also a revolving door: both shown open, separated the guard from the driver.

the entire front of the coach and its appearance can perhaps only be established by studying photographs. Each train carried the following tools: Westinghouse pipe and spanners; tools; electric lamps; emergency hand lamps; hand pumps; fire extinguishers; fuses.

The coaches were numbered 3201–3224 in sequence with the first-class centre coaches being numbered 3202/5/8/3211/4/7/3220/3. The other coaches were the motor thirds. At some point in their early career the actual units were numbered 1E–8E, although, as already mentioned, all coaches were loose coupled. The unit numbers were at one stage applied centrally between the forward-facing cab windows. There is pictorial evidence that the units operated trial services in the original three-car formations without the unit numbers so they can only have been carried for a short period as they were dropped when the units were re-formed (see below). Presumably there were fairly regular reformations to meet the exigencies of the service and indeed this applied to all LB&SCR stock. The coaches were completed sometime before being required and were stored at the request of the LB&SCR by Metropolitan until delivered – the delayed launch date mentioned earlier might be linked to this arrangement. The stock was later known as the 'SL' stock.

One aspect not achieved in the original plans was the take-up of first-class travel. It was probably assumed that a large number of former second-class passengers would move up the scale – but inevitably they traded down and there was a conspicuous excess of first-class accommodation. The comparative luxury of the third-class coaches perhaps contributed to this, although Brown identifies that the first-class users who had led the move to the suburbs in the 1850–80 period were probably now retiring and being replaced by younger and therefore less well-off travellers.

Within a very short period the decision was taken to eliminate a significant proportion of the surplus first-class accommodation by providing replacement driving trailer composite coaches and the sets were re-formed into two-car units. As the trailer-first coaches had no handbrake and needed a lot less maintenance than the motor coaches there were regular re-formations, which operationally required special care with scotching of the trailers, etc. These first-class coaches were reused elsewhere as steam-hauled stock after being fitted with two lavatories in the centre bay, each with access from four compartments, together with removal of the electrical wiring, etc. The rebuilt coaches were renumbered 167 to 174 and were used on London to Brighton mainline services, which had the same width restrictions as 'City Limited' stock. Renumbered Nos 7644–51 by the Southern Railway, they later returned to electric service on the third rail network, although significantly rebuilt.

The replacement driving trailer composite coaches were 48ft long (although one source says 47ft 11in) and 8ft wide over body panels, 51ft 7in over buffers and 8ft 9in over handles. The two first-class compartments were each 6ft wide behind the driver's compartment and the six second-class compartments had a width of 5ft 2.625in and weighed 20 tons. These were not fitted with a gangway as they were narrower than the original stock. The seating capacity was sixteen first class and sixty second class.

These coaches were not new, being converted from locomotive-hauled Brake Thirds (originally constructed by Birmingham Railway Carriage and Wagon Co or Brighton Works) at Lancing Works of the LB&SCR. These coaches were originally seven-compartment 'Bogie Block' brake thirds. Six compartments were retained at the inner end. The seventh compartment and the brake van were rebuilt into the two first-class compartments and the driver's compartment. The first-class compartments were adjacent to the driving compartment. Thereafter, in each two-car unit the seating capacity was sixteen first and probably 126 second class. Howard Turner implies that the motor coaches were fitted with 150hp motors at this time although this seems unlikely – after all the equipment was fairly new and the power to weight ratio was only marginally worse in the two-coach as opposed to three-coach units – is any reader able to offer clarification on these points? It has been noted that the motors fitted to the later 'CP' stock were interchangeable with the earlier type, so perhaps it was possible to uprate the earlier type through modification at a relatively low cost.

The coaches converted in 1910 were numbered 3225–3230. The 1911 batch conversion was numbered 4057–4060 and the final 1912 batch was 4065–4068. The intermediate numbers were occupied by other electric stock (see the next part of this series). Sources agree that most of the coaches were converted at Lancing, although there are suggestions that the last two were converted by the Birmingham Railway Carriage and Wagon Co. For operational reasons, all the original motor coaches were organised to face Victoria, the new trailers facing London Bridge.

Those who can count will note that there were only fourteen converted trailer coaches and that there were originally sixteen motor coaches! The official allocation at this stage was thirteen two-coach units plus three spare motors and one spare trailer. The re-formed units were painted all over umber, the original motor coaches simply having the upper panels painted over. The discrepancy in style between the original motor coaches and the replacement trailers was quite marked. The unit numbers were no longer used after re-formation, although they had been physically eliminated prior to this.

An additional jumper socket (making three) was fitted to vehicle ends for control connections and was mounted about 18ft above the buffer beam. In addition, a hose to enable connections of the main reservoir equalising pipe was added, leading to a total of six physical connections required between units. This arrangement was perpetuated on later AC stock.

During the period while the rebuilt driving trailers were being converted, some of the driving trailer composites ordered for the Crystal Palace electrification (again see next part of this series) were probably utilised on South London line services.

The SL coaches acquired headcodes in the form of 'SL' between the forward-facing cab windows from April 1925, although the Carriage Working Appendices referred to them as

A final view of No. 3203 again, clearly posed, as the service would, according to the position of the 'LV' flag and direction of the bow, be due to head away from the photographer. Was the LBSCR overhead catenary wire fitted so as to move slightly from side to side – as per current practice – intended to even out wear on the bow?

'two-coach motor sets'. Two further driving trailer coaches were added to the South London allocation in 1921, presumably as a result of much greater demand in the peak after the war. The SR renumbered the motor coaches 8601–16 and the trailers to 9811–24. Most of the stock was repainted in Southern Railway lined olive green with unlined green for the coach ends. All thirty vehicles were withdrawn on 17 June 1928 and subsequently modified for DC usage, which we shall cover later.

References:

Southern Electric by G.T. Moody (Fifth Edition) published by Ian Allan.

The London Brighton & South Coast Railway, Vol. III by J. Howard Turner, published by Batsford.

The London Brighton and South Coast Railway by C. Hamilton Ellis, published by Ian Allan.

The Carriage Stock of the LB&SCR by P. Newbury, published by Oakwood Press.

Bogie Carriages of the London, Brighton & South Coast Railway by David Gould, published by Oakwood Press.

Southern Electric, Vol. 1 by David Brown, published by Capital Transport.

A Pictorial Record of Southern Electric Units by Brian Golding, published by Noodle Books.

London's Elevated Electric Railway by Geoff Goslin, published by Connor & Butler.

Reference to *The Brighton Circular*, published by the Brighton Circle, has also provided invaluable material.

Railway South East, Vol. 3 No. 1 has a history of the South London line by H.P. White.

In addition *Live Rail* has provided material – the articles of S.C.W.S..

www.bloodandcustard.com/slac.html John Atkinson, C. Watts.

Colour Interlude

W ith the opportunity presented to include a selection of what we believe are previously unseen colour images ... well we could hardly refuse.

Above: **We start this small treasure trove of colour with this view of No. 30855** *Robert Blake* **slowly negotiating the curves of the Western Docks at Southampton with the** *Andes* **(Royal Mail Line) boat train of Sunday, 16 April 1961. In the Special Traffic Notice for the day, the service is shown as leaving Waterloo at 9.10 am, and was allowed a leisurely ninety-three minutes to pass Southampton Central (booked local line) and a further twelve minutes for the remaining short distance to destination in what were the New Docks. Unfortunately we are not, unusually, told of the formation but it certainly looks interesting, with Maunsell stock, a downgraded and repainted Pullman serving as a buffet car, green Mk1 vehicles and then at least one Pullman in correct company colours. The schedule shows the engine returned light to Eastleigh leaving at 11.15 and was allowed twenty-eight minutes to reach the depot.** *Tony Molyneaux*

Opposite top: **Two-car 'Hampshire' unit No. 1101 standing at what was then platform 2 at Eastleigh. No date; but probably very early in the 1960s as this was one of the sets augmented to three cars soon into their lives. The train is probably an Alton line service. Just ahead of the front car was one of the two large board crossings between the platforms – a further one may be seen some distance ahead. The banner repeaters were installed in the 1950s at the time the top co-acting arms were removed from the up starting signals and with the lower arms otherwise invisible until passing under the station footbridge. Maintenance of these repeaters was, of course, necessary from time to time, hence a walkway was provided on the outside of the bridge leading back to the main building.** *Tony Molyneaux*

Bottom: **Making a cautious approach around the sharp curve to St Denys, No. 34015** *Exmouth* **with a coastway working.**

Above: **Strange bed fellows at Eastleigh, although some might rightly say they represent two of the ugliest design steam engines ever built. The former 'Crosti'-boilered '9F', No. 92028 has arrived at Eastleigh for works attention at a time in the early 1960s when Eastleigh had spare capacity for overhauling steam. The 'Crosti' would have been towed south as it will be noted the connecting rods have been removed. Even so and with the wheels still in balance this would likely have been a night-time move as there would have been a slow maximum speed limit – probably 20mph. The engine lasted in service on the LMR until the end of 1966.**

Opposite: **Still with Southampton Docks for a moment, this was the signal controlling access back on to the main line north at Canute Road crossing – for the Eastern Docks – and was operated from the appropriately named Canute Road crossing seen just beyond the closed gate. In the heyday of the boat trains, two lines were available from here through to Northam Junction and beyond, but rationalisation has taken its toll and here in September 1981 just one remained – hence the bracket signal has also lost an arm.** *Tony Molyneaux*

Also at rest at Eastleigh, this time on 11 May 1963, was No. 34105 *Swanage*. Typical 1960s condition – it would get a lot worse later – AWS fitted, a number of understandable 'bent and bashed' bits, but with a tender full of coal otherwise seemingly serviced and ready to be lit up and go. In the background, the 'USA' tanks are on what was known as the 'Works' or 'Scrap' road. *Tony Molyneaux*

One of the four massive 'G16' 4-8-0 tank engines introduced in 1921 specifically for shunting at the Feltham hump yard. No. 30495 is at Eastleigh on an unreported date and, from the fresh paint applied to the smokebox it could have been in for an 'Intermediate' overhaul. Whatever, this would undoubtedly have been its last works visit as it had ceased work by the end of 1962 and was cut up at Eastleigh just one month later.

Above: **Hidden away on a siding at the back of the shed in May 1966 was this snow plough, the lower portion of which had originally seen service as a loco tender, from a 'Schools'. The Southern converted several former 'Schools' locomotive tenders for departmental use circa 1964, most of this work being undertaken at Ashford.**

Right: **To the south-west now, and one of the last strongholds of the 'T9s', Wadebridge. Here No. 30717 is waiting, possibly to head west to journey's end of the SR at Padstow on 16 July 1960. As it is summer, the steam heat hose has also been removed from the front of the engine. No. 30717 had a little over a year to survive and was withdrawn at the end of July 1961.** *Roger Thornton*

From the express type of the start of the twentieth century to the final express design for the Southern, represented here by rebuilt 'Merchant Navy' No. 35022 *Holland America Line*, awaiting its next duty at Bournemouth shed. This was also a Bournemouth-based engine and would spend most of its time working between Waterloo and Bournemouth/Weymouth. *W. Kellaway*

To the South Eastern, and a 4-SUB passing the car sheds at Orpington in 1962. Headcode '70' indicates either a Charing Cross to Dartford via Bexley Heath service, or a Victoria–Orpington or Sevenoaks via Herne Hill and Petts Wood working. Might the alternate white/black colouring on the side be the remnant of a Second World War camouflage paint scheme?

Eastleigh on 14 March 1966 with the two types of 'HA' electro-diesels at rest outside the steam shed. Leading is No. E6003 of the first batch of six, while behind is one of the subsequent build of a further forty-three and also displaying corporate blue livery. Note the different designs of buffers.

On 18 June 1966, this member of the D65xx class (later Class 33) was captured at Worting Junction with a train of condemned vehicles on their way to scrap. The direction of travel is unusual as the train is heading east having come off the West of England line – the Bournemouth line coming down off its flyover in the background. The consist is not confirmed, but visually at least it appears to be a pair of 'PAN' motor cars, followed by an SECR brake third. The LMR livery van may have been part of the train or simply there to act in a brake capacity. *Les Elsey*

'Happenstance'

Alastair Wilson

Above and page 44: 'Pomp and Circumstance' at Victoria!*. **Finding images of the special trains involved in Alastair's article have, not surprisingly, turned out to be impossible – so far. What we have instead are three images from an album purchased from the estate of the late R.C. Riley some years ago, showing the preparations for special workings at Victoria. Agreed all are some years before the events described in the article and show the LBSCR side of the station, but as far as we know they are all previously unseen and do indicate the effort the railway companies went to when arranging a special working. (Pity the ordinary passenger perhaps having his regular journey disrupted in consequence.) The first and second images show the station decorated for the departure of the Shah on 5 July 1873. Then, twenty-eight years later we have a view of the station ready for the reception of Their Royal Highnesses the Duke and Duchess of Cornwall and York, 2 November 1901.** (**we accept that this particular piece by Sir Edward Elgar was not composed until 1904.*)

At the start of my comments in *SW45* on the article in *SW44* that reproduced the report on the possible acquisition by the Southern of the West Sussex Railway (also known locally as the 'Selsey Tram'), I wondered out loud if anyone knew how it was that the report's writer, E.C. Cox, had been awarded the MVO (Member of the Royal Victorian Order). I think that by sheer pure happenstance, I may be able to answer my own question.

I had also noted that awards to the various grades of the Royal Victorian Order were in the gift of the Sovereign and were nothing to do with the government. I remarked that the type of work for the Sovereign that might result in an award could include organising a major railway journey for royalty. I believe that I was nearer the mark than I knew.

Here followeth a digression – my apologies, but it just shows how successful research can sometimes be the result of a series of happy accidents.

I have subscribed to the *Railway Magazine* since July 1949, and have a complete bound run from that time, to date: I have also collected a substantial number of bound volumes from earlier years, so that I now have about two-thirds of the run from 1921 to June 1949. Ten months ago, I was with my family in London, in St Martin's Lane, and was hanging around outside a shop, inside which my granddaughter was being fitted for a pair of ballet shoes (definitely *not* my kind of shopping). I strolled along to the shop round the corner, which happened to be a print-seller's, and outside it had books for sale. And there were a number of bound volumes of the *Railway Magazine* including Volume 1, for 1897. Well, naturally I pounced. Enquiries inside the shop revealed that the print-seller had a continuous run of thirty half-yearly bound volumes of the *Railway Magazine* – to the end of 1912 – all in what book-sellers would classify as 'near-fine' condition, and all uniformly bound in leather, except for Volume 1, which was in a different binding, and in no more than 'good' condition. The print seller was selling them cheaply because he had only bought them to cannibalise them for the F. Moore coloured prints that had been loose inserts for many early issues. Well, it would have been nice to have had the F. Moores, but most have been reproduced elsewhere and I've probably seen them, or got them in one or other of my books: what I wanted was the magazine and its text and illustrations. So, for about the price of one month's 2017 *Railway Magazine,* I got six months of priceless railway history – just over two years' 2017 subscription got me fifteen years of the earliest *Railway Magazines* in excellent condition.

Well, 'Lucky old you', you may say – or even 'Jammy *******', what's that got to do with Mr Cox, the SR's Traffic Manager in 1934, and his MVO? This is where we come to the second bit of happenstance, and, I hope, matters that are more likely to be of interest to readers of *Southern Way*.

Having got this treasure trove, I have been going through the volumes as reading in bed material, dipping into articles that caught my interest. I am currently on Volume 27 (July–December 1910) and there, I think I have found the answer to my question about Cox's MVO.

As I was turning the pages, my eye was caught by a nice portrait of GWR No. 4021, *King Edward*, then just over a year old, prepared for working the Royal funeral train from Paddington to Windsor, carrying the coffin of King Edward VII. The image was at the head of an article in the July 1910 issue, entitled 'A Record in Royal Specials' and I settled down to read it, because the words 'South Eastern and Chatham' caught my eye and our editor is always complaining that *SW* doesn't get enough SECR/Eastern Section material. The article stated that the SECR had 'brought to London and carried back more than 80 ruling monarchs, crown princes, special envoys and ambassadors'.

Edwin Charles Cox, 1868–1958. Later Traffic Manager Southern Railway, also a lieutenant colonel in the Engineer and Railway Staff Corps. His portrait dates from 1928.

The King had died on 6 May, aged 69. The funeral took place on 20 May. As for the specials, 'the first of these was provided on 8 May and from that date almost every day witnessed one or more royal specials … The record was reached on 18 May when no fewer than seven special trains had to be provided to Victoria.' Victoria was the preferred terminus because it was the closest to Buckingham Palace.

There followed a list of the specials and who was in them, as tabulated below – to our generation the list of passengers will seem Ruritanian (see page 45).

(see page 45)

In addition to the appropriate Royal 'greeter' (King George V himself met the Kaiser, the King of Portugal and the King of the Belgians; the late King's brother, the Duke of Connaught, met most of the rest) and the Foreign Officer representative, each special was met at Victoria by the Chairman of the SECR Managing Committee, Cosmo Bonsor, and the General Manager, while the Superintendent of the Line or one of his officers travelled on each train. Mr E.C. Cox was one of the latter, and it would have been for that that he got his MVO. Phew! At last!

After the funeral, all the Royals had to be taken back by special train, mostly to Dover, the last ones leaving on 30 May. So between 8 May and 30 May, the red carpet on the Chatham

Port	Time of Departure	Make-up of Train	Passengers
Folkestone	1.20 pm	Not stated	Duke of Aosta (Nephew of the King of Italy)
Dover (Admiralty Pier)	3.00 pm	Five bogie half-saloons	Crown Prince of Roumania Prince Maximilian of Baden Grand Duke of Hesse Prince Philip of Saxe-Cobourg Prince Leopold of Saxe-Cobourg
Dover (Prince of Wales Pier)	3.10 pm	Bogie brake saloon Royal saloon Bogie corridor first	King of Portugal Crown prince of Servia
Dover (Admiralty Pier)	3.30 pm	Not stated	M Stephen Pichon – French Foreign Minister and French Mission Turkish Mission Chinese Mission
Dover (Prince of Wales Pier)	5.00 pm	Not stated	King of the Belgians Prince Rupert of Bavaria
Port Victoria	5.15 pm	Not stated	Prince Henry of the Netherlands
Not stated (Probably Dover)	5.30 pm	Not stated	Prince Fushima of Japan Grand Duke of Mecklenburg-Strelitz Prince Charles of Sweden

On the next day, 19 May, the following specials were run:

Port	Time of Departure	Make-up of Train	Passengers
Queenborough Pier		Not stated Ordinary train to Herne Hill, thence special to Victoria	Prince John George of Saxony
Queenborough Pier	Same time	Half-saloon direct to Victoria	Princess Ellen of Greece
Port Victoria	10.30 am	SECR Royal Train	Kaiser Wilhelm of Germany & Suite
Folkestone Pier	1.40 pm	Saloon attached to ordinary train	Prince Bovarady of Siam
Dover (Prince of Wales Pier)	3.00 pm	Not stated	King of Bulgaria Prince George of Montenegro Persian Mission
Folkestone (town)	3.30 pm	Saloon attached to ordinary train to Charing Cross	Count d'Eu Prince Pierre (the Comte d'Eu was the consort of the pretender to the throne of Brazil – she was a relative of King Edward VII
Dover	3.30 pm	Not stated	Archduke Franz Ferdinand of Austria Duke Albrecht of Wurtemberg

side of Victoria must have been rolled and unrolled over and over again, while the cleaning gangs at Dover, Faversham and Stewarts Lane, to say nothing of the carriage cleaners, would have been cleaning and polishing Harry Wainwright's 'Ds' and 'Es' to within an inch of their lives, and superb they must have looked in all the glory of that most flashy of locomotive liveries. The *Railway Magazine* article also records that Kaiser Wilhelm left a tip of £20 (the equivalent of £2,290 in 2018 money) for the officials and train crews involved.

And the arrangements weren't all SECR and royalty – the article also records that the LSWR moved 10,000 troops to London (and back again) for street-lining parties and marching contingent!

Joseph 'Jock' Callaghan
Station Master Waterloo

With the help also of John Burgess, we were recently passed a small amount of papers from the archive of the late Joseph 'Jock' Callaghan, who at the end of his career achieved the pinnacle of every lad-porter's dream – that of station master and then area manager at one of the big London Termini – in his case, and as the title of this article implies, at Waterloo.

Mr Callaghan though was not one who commenced his railway career as a management trainee and instead he climbed his way up from humble beginnings as a signal box lad on the LNER at Thornton Junction north of Edinburgh. His was also a railway family with his father a guard and his brother a driver.

His papers include a very brief handwritten note of his 'postings' and career, and although all 'non-Southern' apart

Joseph (third from left) accompanying the then Chairman of British Rail, Sir Peter Parker (second from left), at Waterloo sometime between 1976 and 1979. This may well be related to the view.

from the final entry, do make for interesting reading:

8-4-35 – Signal Box lad, Thornton Junction (One item in the file refers to 1934)

Sept 1935 – redundant but soon after reinstated to same position

Feb 1939 – Porter Signalman, Leith Walk

Apr 1939 – Signalman, Buckhaven

16-10-39 – Called to arms, being part of the BEF and evacuated from Le Havre in 1940. Rose to become a CSM in the Black Watch serving in Gibraltar and North Africa. (No doubt his regimental training helped as in photographs he is recorded as standing ramrod straight!)

11-3-46 – Re-joined the LNER as District Relief Signalman, Thornton

25-10-46 – Temporary position as Signalman, Thornton South signal box

14-1-47 – Signalman, Thornton North

14-3-47 – Signalman, Neasden North

24-3-47 – Signalman, Belle Vue, Kings Cross

Appointed to Special Class Signalman Neasden South but never took over

3-11-47 – Class 5 Clerk, Ferne Park Sidings

Jan/Feb 1949 – St Ronans BR Clerical Training School, Hadley Wood

24-3-49 – School of signals Hatfield

16-5-49 – Class 5 Summer relief station master

26-9-49 – Class 4 Clerk, Kings Cross

? – Class 4 Station Master

16-11-53 – Class 3 District Inspector, Kings Cross

8-9-54 – Class 2 District Inspector, Hitchin

20-7-57 – Class 1 District Inspector, Kings Cross

1958 – Elected Associate Member IRSE

3-10-59 – 'Special A' Line Manager, Liverpool Street

? – Special B' Yard Master, Ferme Park

? – MS1 Assistant to District Superintendent

Dec 1963 – MS2 Deputy Station Master, Kings Cross

Sept 1965 – MS4 Area Manager, Marylebone

? – MS5 Outdoor Assistant to the General Manager ER

? – MS5 Operating Officer, Euston

17-5-71 – Station Manager/Area Manager, Waterloo

30-6-79 – Retired aged 60, having been a long term member of the TSSA

Joseph Callaghan depicted 'while climbing the slippery pole of promotion'. When interviewed later in his career and asked how he had worked his way up, he responded, 'It is only through sheer hard work and a whole lot of luck that I have managed to move up the ladder to such a high step.' This and the accompanying images and paperwork were found amongst his effects and consequently we have no idea as to a location or date.

Sir Peter, Joseph and other dignitaries on a visit to the Waterloo signal box.

The family papers contain a wealth of newspaper cuttings, mostly undated and almost without exception all from his time on the Southern but (and despite this being the *Southern Way*,) nothing in the way of notes reporting events from earlier in his career. They would surely have made for fascinating reading.

The new man at Waterloo was also very much in the public eye of both the national daily and the London evening papers, as well as the railway staff publications, and consequently we see several snippets of Joseph having been interviewed and quoted, 'When you see me on the platform with my claymore and kilt you will know it really has gone wrong' – *there is no record we ever did!* When questioned on his own career he added, 'It is only through sheer hard work and a whole lot of luck that I have managed to move up the ladder to such a high step.' Another, this time a newspaper reporter's headline provided a flashback to his time as a company sergeant major, 'Step lively you miserable trains … what are you? A useless, idle shower of carriages.' When appointed and asked as to his aims, Joseph stated, 'I am going to make timekeeping my priority. At the present 80–85% of trains to Waterloo run on time, 90% would be a good target. I shall make a careful assessment of the present situation and if I find anything

needs to change I shall look for the best way of changing it.'

Not timekeeping related, but we know that one of his first tasks at Waterloo was to speed up the arrival of two £7,000 cleaning machines to sweep and vacuum the platforms and also scrub with soap and water as well. His justification was, 'A clean station shows pride in the job – like neat and tidy uniforms.'

Slightly different (perhaps exaggerated figures) were used in various press reports but when interviewed in 1971 the press stated he was in charge of both Waterloo and Waterloo East, handling 200,000 and 30,000 passengers respectively, each daily. There were also a reported 1,500 staff at the two stations. Joseph was a commuter himself, living at Leatherhead and coming in to his office daily by train.

Interviewed later in his office near Platform 16, he commented, 'Waterloo is a round-the-clock operation. It is of course a very heavy commuter station but it also has two other faces; it caters for the main line passengers to the West Country and the South Coast by Inter-City trains. During the night hours, the station changes its complex to become an intensive parcels operation, together with a very heavy newspaper concentration until approximately 4.00 am.'

This was likely to have been around the mid-point of his Waterloo posting, as the report went on to describe seeing Mr Callaghan darting from one end of the concourse to the other collecting tickets and advising would-be travellers puzzled by the black notice boards. When questioned he commented, 'I've never been a ticket collector but my job today is to keep the whole thing going and do the jobs where people have failed to turn up.' (Whether this was due to bad weather or some form of industrial action was not commented upon.)

Probably a while later, an extended feature in one of railway staff magazines covered both Mr Callaghan and improvements at Waterloo that were due to take place some years before the major upgrade for the Channel Tunnel trains. It was headed, 'Ray Lowther goes behind the scenes at Britain's busiest rail terminal'. The article, reproduced below, also provides us with a useful view of the then contemporary station and included a number of headline facts.

Alastair Wilson also adds the following: 'Between 1972 and 1974; and again 1977-1979, I commuted into Waterloo on a daily and later weekly basis. A feature of Waterloo in the morning rush hour was indeed the playing over the loudspeaker system of martial marches. I had understood that it was to encourage the crowds to "step lively", and so

clear the station area as quickly as possible. Was it even Mr. Callaghan's army training which gave him the idea of introducing this feature? I know I unconsciously stepped out in time with the music … .'

Waterloo is British Rail's busiest terminal station. Each weekday it handles 1,200 trains and around 181,000 passengers – almost double the size of a Wembley Cup Final crowd.

It is the mainstay of the commuter scene and in the heaviest single hour of the peak between 8.15 and 9.15 in the mornings – 41,000 people arrive at the station.

There may be those among the rail enthusiasts who will be quick to reflect that Waterloo lacks the glamour services associated with some other London termini – there is no 'Flying Scotsman' as at Kings Cross, no 125 miles-an-hour High Speed Trains like those which leave Paddington for the West Country and Wales; no 'Clansman to the Scottish Highlands or 'Royal Scot|' to Glasgow which give added colour to Euston; no 'Night Ferry', the international sleeping car service to Brussels and Paris which helps to mark Victoria's link with the continent and no 'Hook Continental' or 'Day Continental' which underline Liverpool Street's connections with Holland and other European countries. Liverpool Street, incidentally with 151,000 passengers a day, is British Rail's second busiest station.

One of the duties of the station master was to greet VIP travellers. Here Joseph is seen with HM Queen Elizabeth on the occasion of a royal journey by rail. Perhaps slightly interesting is that there is no red carpet, while in years past the bowler would instead have been a top hat.

But even the purists in the ranks of the enthusiasts will readily admit that Waterloo, with its hustle and bustle, its twenty-one platforms, its constant arrivals and departures and its own underground link to the Bank, is good bread and butter railway operating – and good railway service. The man responsible for ensuring the achievement and maintenance of those high standards is Mr Joe Callaghan, the area manager. A down-to-earth Scot, he began his career as a booking lad in the signal box at Thornton Junction, Fife back in 1935.

Waterloo is on a 24 acre site and Mr Callaghan has a total of 800 staff under his control. They include commercial and movement assistants and also five station managers who rotate on 24-hour coverage of the whole area which extends to Queens Road – two and three-quarter miles down the line. There are administration, parcels, ticket issuing and travel centre staff, supervisors, chargemen, platform and parcels staff, as well as train guards.

What is it like to run an organisation of that kind? Mr Callaghan seated in his office near platform 16, told me, 'The most important factor is the arrangements for the platform workings.

'This is pre-planned by the central timing office in the general manager's building on the station, in conjunction with my movements clerks.'

He continued, 'However, there are daily planned alterations owing to various aspects such as engineers' occupation or additional trains. These are programmed by the movements clerks.'

On top of that, there are many unscheduled changes which have to be made because of such factors as defective stock, points or signal failures, late running or shortage of train crews. These problems have to be dealt with on the spot by the signal box regulator and the station supervisor, who is housed in an office which overlooks the main line platforms.

There are only eight lines (four up and four down) in the throat of Waterloo Station leading to its 21 platforms. In view of the intensity of the service, this in itself presents an operating problem and is something of a brake on flexibility, although Mr Callaghan was swift to point out, 'We can contain the service on the existing layout provided it is closely monitored.'

During the heaviest hour of the morning peak, 64 trains enter the station and 60 leave it.

Mr Callaghan explained, 'The station provides three very distinct services. The suburban side serving mostly the South London and Surrey areas, the main lines covering Surrey, Hampshire and parts of Dorset and Wiltshire; and the Windsor lines which serve some of the Thames Valley and Berkshire. There has to be close cooperation in the working of these three functions and this is contained between the signal box and my supervisors'

The Waterloo electric-powered signal box – situated just outside the platform area – is of the miniature lever frame type. The 307 levers cover 71 points and 194 signals. Staffed by twelve signalmen and two regulators – with a peak of five at one time – the box contains four illuminated track diagrams. These are suspended from the ceiling over the levers, which are laid out at waist level. This signal box is due for replacement by the most modern type of panel box in the mid-1980s.

`Most of the rolling stock is stabled at Clapham Junction and Wimbledon Park but overnight trains are kept in the station platform roads for the early morning services. Apart from at the peak period, all trains are swept out at Waterloo and the main line stock is cleaned and serviced. Mr Callaghan said: 'We do as much interior cleaning as time permits. The average time available, outside the peak, for cleaning is fifteen minutes, which allows time for passengers to leave the train and also makes it available for passengers to board the train at least five minutes before its departure.'

At one time, Waterloo was renowned for its boat trains to Southampton which connected with the big luxury Atlantic liners. But today, a mere trickle of that traffic remains, compared with the past – only cruise liners like the *Oriana*. *Canberra* and the *QE2* survive to give an occasional reminder of how things used to be.

Last year we did see the beginning of a new maritime venture, when three Russian cruising ships – the *Taros Sherchenko*, the *Leonid Sobinov* and the *Mikhail Lermontov* – included a call at Southampton and were provided with a boat train service from Waterloo.

For seven months of the year, there are regular daily boat train departures from Waterloo to Weymouth for the Sealink sailing to Cherbourg and the Channel Islands. In keeping with the times, Waterloo provides a fast rail service to Feltham, where there is a connecting bus link to Heathrow. There is also an hourly service to Southampton Airport, for flights to the Channel Islands.

One somewhat unusual but traditional service in which Waterloo plays a big part is British Rail's only underground railway – the line to the Bank. Affectionately called 'The Drain' this conjures up visions of city gents in bowler hats, urgently scanning the columns of their copies of the *Financial Times*. It us not quite like that nowadays but the trains still run fully packed at three to four minute intervals during the morning and evening peak periods – and carry twelve million passengers a year. Mr Callaghan said: 'We have a total of five five-car trains allotted to this service. They are custom built – very similar in style to the London Transport Underground trains.'

Serving as it does, some popular seaside resorts. Waterloo has its constant invasion of holidaymakers, from Easter onwards. 'We run considerably more additional trains on summer Saturdays and in order to contain the flows of passengers to each destination. We resort to organised queuing on the concourse, away from the barrier gates.

Mr Callaghan has been area manager at the station for seven-and-a-half years and was able to say. 'We work as a team and we can cope with the crowds.'

'We had a new ticket office opened in 1970 and this has sixteen hooking windows and is really designed to cope with the heaviest flow. The balance of the manning is geared to meet the passenger flow but all windows are fully manned on Friday afternoons and on peak Saturday mornings.'

Another regular duty for the station master was to attend retirement presentations and there are several such views of these within the family archive. Unfortunately no names are mentioned. This one though is perhaps slightly special as it appears to be Joseph's own send-off, the decanter seemingly just one of several farewell gifts; another of which was a greenhouse (established by studying the illustrations on either end of the presentation table!).

Below the station is an extensive parcels complex covering 'Called For', 'Despatch' and a cross-London road service between the London termini.

Much of the parcels traffic is moved during the night and Waterloo also plays its part in the 'Red Star' countrywide express service.

All told, Waterloo handles some six-and-a-half million parcels a year. The parcels organisation is not the only feature under the concourse and platforms at Waterloo. Gloria Pearson, a Southern Region public relations officer summed up the situation very adequately when she told me, 'It is like a hidden city – another world – under Waterloo'. 'We have got the parcels activity with vans coming and going; there is a labyrinth of tunnels and arches used as wine cellars by commercial firms, a shop selling photographer's equipment, a hairdressers, a gents' tailor and a ladies' outfitters. In addition to all that, the British Transport Hotels have their own wine cellar, sandwich-making department and catering stores for servicing the 'The Trafalgar' and 'The Drum' self service restaurants and their own kiosk on the concourse, as well as the restaurant cars and buffets on the trains'.

Miss Pearson added, 'Our building department has a depot under the station too. Here they have a workshop where they make, amongst other things, office doors – and crossing gates.

And the publicity department's outdoor section prepares beneath the station display boards, publicity material and departure fitments and posters for the region's London termini. Nearby all the publicity posters for the whole region are stocked and despatched from the Bill office.'

If that was not enough to indicate the variety of life under Waterloo, Then Miss Pearson's final words sealed the scene. 'Oh, I've forgotten the archway full of fresh eggs. This is used by Stonegate, the egg distributor.' *(But no mention of the 'Plan Arch' where many researchers spend many a happy hour entertained by Reg, Derek, Bill etc ... Ed.)*

Overlooking and bordering the main concourse are the four floors of offices used as the headquarters of the Region's general manager.

In the basement of these offices is a section of staff whose top-quality work often helps to brighten the pages of this newspaper and many other publications – an arm of British Rail's Central Photographic Unit.

On the concourse is the Lost Property Office which caters for the whole region. Each year it handles something like 70,000 articles, ranging over a wide variety of belongings from the inevitable umbrellas and gloves, to things like a policeman's helmet, a wedding dress, and even false teeth.

In 1977 the station received a major boost with the opening of a new Travel Centre – the first on British Rail premises to incorporate a London Transport enquiry office. Housed in what used to be the Windsor Tearoom, the Southern Region architects retained some of the old features such as the Ionic Columns, fluted pilasters and mirrors in the new attractive décor.

Mr Callaghan informed me, 'Since the travel centre has opened, receipts have rocketed.'

Last year marked a big step in the modernisation of Waterloo with the completion of a facelift which cost over half-a-million pounds.

Waterloo manager retires

NOW enjoying a far more restive life of retirement in the peace and quietness of Fetcham, near Leatherhead in Surrey is Mr Joe Callaghan who, until July, was the area manager at Waterloo.

Mr Callaghan, was a member of the T.S.S.A. Southern Region Management Staff Branch.

Scotsman Joe Callaghan began his railway career as a booking lad in the signal box at Thornton Junction, Fife, on the old London and North Eastern Railway in 1935.

After serving over six years in the famed Black Watch in which he was a sergeant-major, he transferred to King's Cross as a signalman in 1947. Later he became a clerk at Ferme Park and subsequently received several promotions, one of which took him back to Ferme Park as yardmaster. He was operating officer for the London division at Euston before his appointment to the post of area manager at Waterloo in 1971.

Mr Callaghan told the JOURNAL: "I'm going to take

it easy for a while — just doing gardening and decorating."

He added: "Incidentally, I would like to thank the T.S.S.A. for all the good work it did for my colleagues and myself during the time of my railway career. I always found the Association very helpful in all my dealings with it — and I would like also to express my thanks for the retirement cheque which the T.S.S.A. sent me."

Mr Callaghan is succeeded as area manager at Waterloo by Mr Trevor Adams, who was formerly the area manager at Shenfield, on the Eastern Region.

This resulted in the removal of the familiar ornamental gates which clanged so ominously in the face of many a 'last second' passenger, and the disappearance of three wooden train indicator boards, two of which had given information to passengers for over half a century.

The gates have been replaced by a completely new barrier complex with sliding gates which have illuminated indicators above each of them.

Then too, there are three 'Solari' indicator boards containing a much wider range of information than their predecessors. All these are operated simultaneously from the 'nerve centre' – a new office incorporated over the barrier system.

It was here that I spoke to Mr John Lacy one of the five Station Managers who is also the correspondence secretary of the TSSA South Western Depot and Station Managers branch. Messrs Ron Dyer, Norman Fair, Tom Henningsen and Bert Little are also in the TSSA.

Mr Lacy informed me, 'This modernisation has resulted in much more effective control of the station. Before this communications were difficult between key staff because of their scattered locations. Now with the indicator, the operators and announcer are in the same office as the main station supervisor and have a direct telephone link to every ticket barrier – the public can be more readily informed when things go wrong.

'It all helps us on the operating side because we can quickly contact the staff.'

Mr Lacy continued, 'The other big factor we have secured through this new set up is having at our finger tips an indication of when trains are ready to depart and that the signalman has cleared the signal for departure. We even have television to give a view of certain platforms and the concourse.

'Our control room is hooked into the signalling system. This means that whilst it does not work the signalling system, the control directs the station working from up-to-the-minute information it receives through its links with the signal box and the divisional train control at Wimbledon.

'Waterloo has a system in its control room which has also been installed at other locations, basically it enables us to closely monitor the train service.

'We are very conscious of the need to keep the public informed as much as possible. In the control room we can make pre-recorded announcements by a punch-card reader control, make direct announcements and play canned music.

'In effect when using the tapes for the pre-recorded announcements, there is an element of computer technology. This is through the use of a punch-card reader, which is fed by putting a card through an aperture on the desk.

'Before this change, the announcer was confined to straightforward microphone announcing.

'Train departure and arrival indicators are a key factor at any station and Mr Lacy said, 'Our new ones are operated from the control room by one of two punch card readers through a device called a pulse generator which enables the destination flaps on the board to be set as desired.

'Whilst the operation is perhaps no quicker than the old manual one, we can now display train delay information and far more train connecting detail than on the old system.'

The old-fashioned poster board advertising at Waterloo has given way to modern illuminated advertisements over the ticket barrier line and the revenue from these is covering much of the cost of the station renovation.

The renovation has also brought a new look to trading on the station, bright new 'mini-shops' give a more pleasing appearance than the old wooden kiosks which once adorned the concourse.

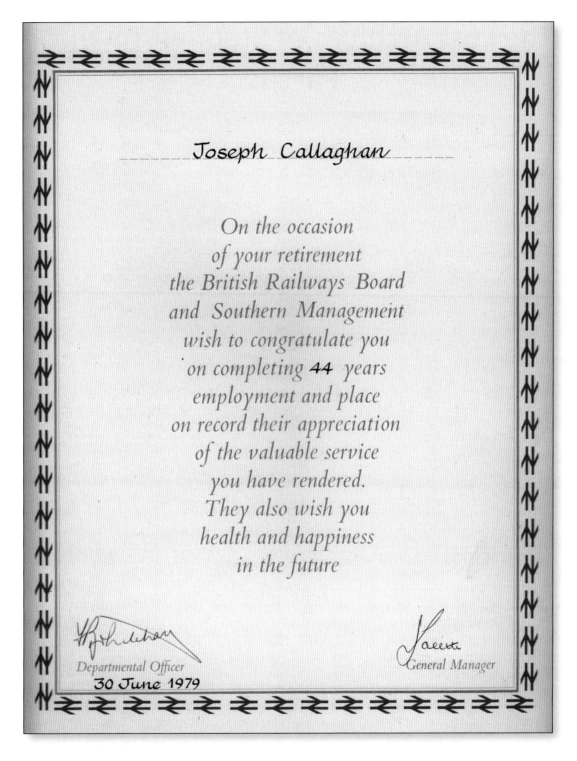

Joseph Callaghan

On the occasion
of your retirement
the British Railways Board
and Southern Management
wish to congratulate you
on completing **44** years
employment and place
on record their appreciation
of the valuable service
you have rendered.
They also wish you
health and happiness
in the future

Departmental Officer
30 June 1979

General Manager

Waterloo of course provides direct interchange facilities to London Transport's Bakerloo and Northern lines. Apart from that and running adjacent to the main station but separated by a cab road and walkway is Waterloo East station.

Situated between Charing Cross and London Bridge, it has four platforms and caters for services to South East London and Kent, thus affording an easy interchange for a variety of routes.

This is controlled by the Station Manager at Charing Cross which is just on the other side of the Thames. Over thirty thousand people use this station every day.

Although train operation is the preoccupation, Waterloo still has time to indulge in a somewhat unique touch – during the early morning rush hour lively tunes are played across the loudspeaker system to cheer the commuters on their way to their office desks, and in the evening there are more soothing notes as they board their trains for home.

So it is not just a station with twenty one platforms, 1,200 trains a day and its own underground line – but seemingly a place with a heart.

Mr Callaghan was succeeded at Waterloo by Trevor Adams.

The Lost Archives of Stephen Townroe
Part 12

As we know, the Southern Railway and its successor, the Southern Region, had a lot of catching up to do post-1945. Arrears of maintenance, rebuilding, new rolling stock and locomotives, and in connection with the latter, some catching up to do on scrapping older machines retained in service for longer due to the needs of the recent past.

Scrapping, nowadays we might more accurately refer to it as reclamation or recycling, was something the railways had been doing since the earliest times. Old rails used for signal posts are perhaps the immediate thought, but look more closely and there are still numerous locations where rails, using the same example, have been utilised to hold back supporting walls and sustain bridges, etc. So far as locomotives were concerned we have already seen within the colour section of this issue an example of a 'Schools' class tender recycled into a snow plough, whilst useful fittings – in steam days basically everything from the boiler, frames, wheel sets, etc – might also be saved to keep other engines in service.

The profusion of Eastleigh views in this instalment of the 'Lost Archives' is simply explained by the fact that SCT had moved to Eastleigh as the man in charge in 1947. (See *Southern Way Special No. 10* for the full biography.) One can almost imagine SCT walking around the depot and its environs, not just with his eye on what was going on but also with camera at the ready. Indeed one former member of the outside depot staff recounted, 'We had to keep at it … we never knew where he might appear from next!'

We start this time with a few examples of engines recorded on the scrap road at Eastleigh in the period 1948/9, continuing with the goings-on at the shed and then conclude with one engine destined to be saved for posterity … (a number of Great Western images in the sequence and involving a footplate trip from the same period have been deliberately omitted.)

Former LBSCR I1X 4-4-2T No. 2597 near the end of its life at Eastleigh. The set of images seen in this selection from SCT were all taken between June 1947 and April 1948. This had been the second member of the twenty-strong class to be laid aside, in December 1946 – notice the condemning 'X; although ten more went in 1948 and the remainder were similarly not long for this world, all succumbing in 1951.

'T3' 4-4-0 No. 571 also on the Eastleigh scrap road, where it had languished since late 1942, some five years or so before this image was taken. This was one of just two members of the class that survived at work into the 1940s, the other being No. 563, of which more anon. Already it has bequeathed parts: at least one clack-valve and the smokebox door handles, while it will be noted the works plate is also missing. Hard to visualise perhaps but in a life of just under fifty years it had accumulated a recorded mileage of 1.778 million miles, equivalent to 35,568 per annum, or likely in excess of 3,000 per week when taking into account 'down time' for works visits, etc. Notice too, evidence of a 'rough-shunt' at the front.

There were several members of the 'B4' class that could be found around Eastleigh, the nearby works having accepted the repair work on the Southampton Docks engines from 1933. The dominance of the class at the docks ended in 1947 with the arrival of the 'USA' class, after which the 'B4s' were scattered far and wide. No. 88, along with sister engine (300)89, being employed for a time shunting the milk siding at Stewarts Lane.

The former Southampton Docks *St Malo*, later from September 1952 BR No. 30093, somewhat dwarfed by the 4-6-0 behind. Someone has added the SR number – 93 – in chalk on the bunker side as well. Bradley records this particular engine having achieved the remarkable record of running 479,905 miles in a career of sixty-eight years, a remarkable figure for an engine that would have spent all its operational life shunting.

'M7' No. 48 on the down main line just south of Eastleigh. This is likely a Southampton Terminus service consisting of a single Maunsell coach with a three-coach LSWR set behind. Of particular interest in this view is the ARP signal box – actually a point box – behind. This controlled a fan of sidings just seen branching out to the left that were provided in the Second World War to stable engines away from the running shed. The houses in the background front Southampton Road while the land on the right is also well cultivated with allotments.

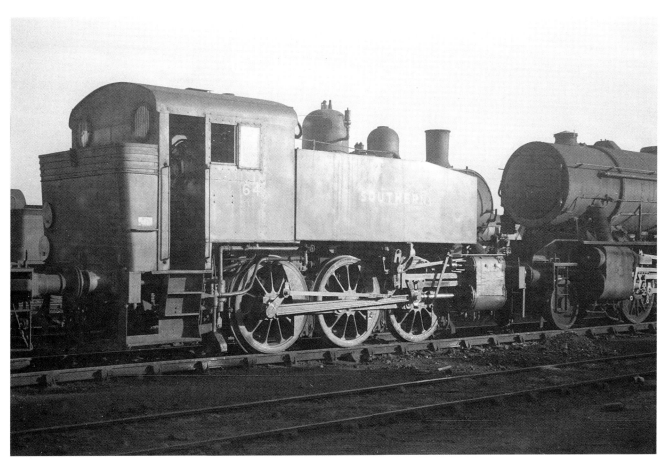

The new order at Southampton Docks. Vulcan-built 0-6-0T WD No. 1959 seen here as Southern Railway No. 64 at Eastleigh and coupled to another stranger in the form of a Riddles design austerity 2-8-0/2-10-0. The photograph shows the engine in near original condition with the small bunker and only a small rooftop cab ventilator.

Another 'B4' with a chalked number identification, No. 102 *Granville* alongside the coal stack at Eastleigh – the roofs of some of the railway houses in Campbell Road are just visible behind. As No. 30102 this engine along with No. 30096 was for many years the regular shunting loco at Winchester City. After BR service, No. 30102 was restored externally and moved to static display at the Butlin's holiday camp at Ayr but was later relocated, again to static display, at Bressingham Hall.

At the rear of the running shed, SCT has recorded oil-burning 'L11' 4-4-0 No. 437. D.L. Bradley has the date of conversion to oil fuel as having been 25 July 1947, and it was also the first of the eight members of the type to be so converted (although the original intention had been to alter fifteen of the class). In its new guise No. 437 was further modified with an electric generator on 10 January 1948, but along with all the others so modified had been laid aside by late September of the same year. It would never work again in any form, although it remained on paper at least 'on the books' until April 1952. It was dismantled at the nearby works.

SR USA No. 70, former WD No. 1960, at Eastleigh and this time modified with an enlarged bunker, increased cab ventilation, and larger rearward facing windows. After sixteen years' service at Southampton Docks, this engine was transferred to Departmental use in August 1963 as DS238 for work at Ashford Wagon Works. It was subsequently saved for preservation on the Kent & East Sussex Railway.

Looking as if it could well be fresh from overhaul, 'Schools' No. 934 *St Lawrence* reposes in the sunshine at the rear of the shed. This was one of twenty of the class modified with a Lemaître blastpipe and wide stovepipe chimney. It was also one of the final batch taken out of service at the time of the 'great cull' on 31 December 1962. A comment in the index refers to the engine as having been newly painted in green livery but, of course, this is not apparent from a head-on view.

Left: Another oil-burning 'L11', this time No. 157, again at Eastleigh. Converted in October 1947 it is reported as having spent much of its time in this guise shunting at Poole. It also had ceased work by the end of September 1948 but was not withdrawn until March 1952.

Below: A final USA, No. 70 again, and complete with all 'outside plumbing'. This is the front of the shed so it may have been that No, 70 has been modified as such at the works – in the background – and has now been worked around to the front of the shed for running-in and then duties at the docks.

No ideas on the location this time but as the next negative in the strip is at Guildford we may assume it may be in the same area. We cannot even say this shows something that on the surface at least is particularly interesting but there again, how many times was such a maintenance issue ever recorded on film?

One of the long-lived members of the 'T9' 4-4-0 type, this one is No. 337, recorded on the turntable at Guildford. No. 337 was one of two members of the class temporarily fitted with speedometers in connection with the running of the air-special: see lead article in *SW43*. Whilst all sixty-six members of the class entered BR service on 1 January 1948, the first inroads into the type were made in 1951–52, although the main cull did not really start until 1957–58 coinciding with the arrival of the new 'Hampshire' DEMU sets. No. 30337 was withdrawn at the end of 1958.

Survivor from another age. One of the two original members of the '415' class, which together with sister engine No. 3125 worked the Lyme Regis branch almost exclusively from 1923 to 1946 when the pair were joined by a third engine, rescued from dereliction on the East Kent Railway. No. 3520 is recorded outside the front of the works at Eastleigh possibly in early 1948. Under BR it was renumbered as 30584 and reappeared in this guise in plain black, although lining was later applied in June 1951. This engine was destined to be the first of the trio to end its service in January 1961 and after a period in store was broken up in December of the same year. It also achieved the remarkable feat of a recorded mileage in excess of 2.1 million miles in seventy-six years, most of that trundling to and fro over the 6½ miles between Axminster and Lyme Regis.

Mention has been made in the past of SCT's 'eye' for framing an image and here we have another example. The main subject is the unidentified 'King Arthur' on the down line passing under Campbell Road bridge just south of Eastleigh – the pair of lines to the right being the entry and exit roads for the running shed. Aside from the fine array of semaphore signals, long replaced by aesthetically inconsequential colour lights, the railwayman walking on the right has to be the making of the view. There was for many years a prohibition notice at the end of the platforms at the nearby station advising footplate staff for the depot that they should use the road to reach the shed, but clearly not all did.

Modernisation in the permanent way department with flat-bottom rail made into a turnout, something we take for granted nowadays but then a recent innovation. The location is again Eastleigh – just north of Bishopstoke bridge – and the rails might well be placed ready for a trial in the roads leaving the east yard before being accepted into main-line use. The 'Q1' is not identified.

A haze of smoke shows the hazard of fire on dry grass. We are not told where, possibly south of Eastleigh, but SCT does note that it was after the passage of a 'Lord Nelson'-hauled train. If we are correct in our assessment of the location then it also goes to show it was not just the locations referred to by Jeffery Grayer in his article earlier in this issue that were at risk.

Below and opposite: Early stages in the restoration of 'T3' No. 563 at Eastleigh. This had been the last survivor of the class, retained for service in the Second World War long after all but one of its classmates had been consigned to history. It too might have suffered the same fate and was indeed taken to Kimbridge Junction (west of Romsey) in January 1948 ready for disposal. Fortunately, before this could commence Eastleigh decided an LSWR engine was required to take part in the centenary celebrations at Waterloo and No. 563 was inspected and chosen to be saved. We can date the image as between January and May of 1948 for at the latter time she entered the works for overhaul, this then is an early stage of stripping and scraping the paintwork prior to entering the works. (More on No. 563, by now restored and in steam, next time.)

Next time in this feature: No. 563, restored and in steam, a 'Remembrance' being coaled, a Beattie 'Well-Tank' fresh from overhaul, and the dangers of a firebox collapse.

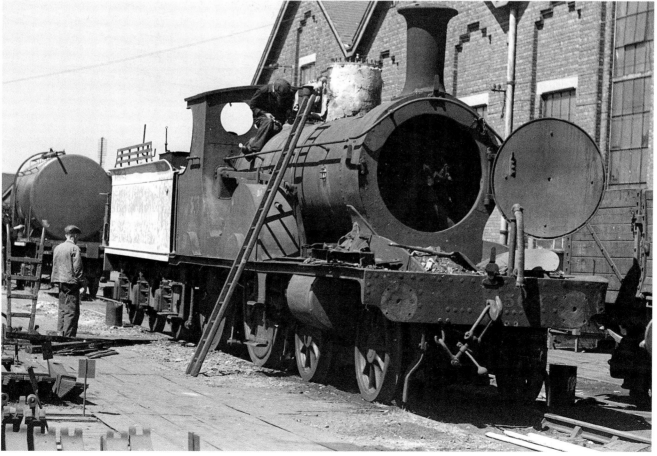

Salisbury–Exeter Part 3

Jeffery Grayer

Time runs out for the old order

To the casual observer in 1963 things were pretty much as usual on the route, steam was still very much in evidence on express and stopping services as well as the various branches that fed from it. However, the multi-portioned holiday trains so characteristic of the route were on borrowed time, such limited date services utilising coaching stock for only a few weeks in the year being anathema to Dr Beeching, whose report was to be published in that year. (Appendix 1 at the end of this article details through workings in 1964, the last summer of steam. Appendix 2 details the number of Pacifics based at Exmouth Junction in 1963 and their subsequent departure. It will be noted that all the Pacifics had been transferred away by September 1964.)

It was apparently the original intention of the WR to use 'Hymeks' on the route but this was amended and once the decision had been taken to use 'Warship' diesels instead, training was organised from 1 June. This generally took place between Salisbury and Basingstoke. It was reported in the *Railway Observer* magazine for May 1964 that 'when diesels are introduced to the Exeter–Salisbury route no new diesel facilities will be constructed on former SR territory, instead the locomotives will be based at sheds that already have diesel maintenance facilities'.

'Merchant Navy' No. 35013 under the coal hopper at Exmouth Junction being prepared for the 'ACE'. *Mark Abbott*

With the brooding presence of Exeter Gaol behind, rebuilt Bulleid Pacific No. 34036 *Westward Ho* has a full head of steam and awaits departure from Exeter Central on a Waterloo service in the dying days of SR steam in 1963. No. 34036 was to remain based at Exmouth Junction shed until October of that year. *Jeffery Grayer*

Also posing beside the massive ferro-concrete coaling chute at Exmouth Junction shed is another 'Merchant Navy' Pacific, No. 35007 *Aberdeen Commonwealth*. Locomotives of this class were the premier motive power of the Exeter line for many years. *Jeffery Grayer*

A third example, No. 35009 *Shaw Savill*, prepares to take over the premier service on the line, the 'Atlantic Coast Express' (ACE), at Exeter Central. Such express workings would soon become a thing of the past under the new semi-fast diesel regime. *Jeffery Grayer*

'72C' Yeovil Town shed, the only intermediate locomotive depot between Salisbury and Exeter, continued to handle steam until its closure in July 1965, having been recoded 83E in September 1963. A variety of motive power is on display here with Nos 34010 *Sidmouth*, 76005, 82011, 31822 and a Prairie tank all awaiting their next turns of duty. *Jeffery Grayer*

Restored to conventional form following experiments with concave smoke deflectors a few years before, No. 34035 *Shaftesbury* is also captured on Yeovil Town shed in early 1963 but was to last for only a few months following the WR takeover and was one of the initial quartet of the class to be withdrawn as early as June 1963: the others were Nos. 34043, 34055 and 34074. *Jeffery Grayer*

By the time No. 34089 *602 Squadron* was photographed on Salisbury shed in 1966 it had, along with many of its classmates, lost its nameplate, badge and smokebox plate. It remained based at Salisbury from September 1963 until the end of SR steam in July 1967.

Upon the boundary change of 1963 that gave control of the line west of Wilton to the Western Region for the first time, steam was still employed on those branch lines that connected with the Salisbury–Exeter main line. Motive power could also vary, from modern-day steam engines of the BR 'Class 4' or 'Class 2' tank engine type (the latter often to be seen on the Sidmouth Junction–Exmouth via Tipton, and Exeter–Exmouth direct serves respectively, to more venerable motive power on other branch line services. Here push-pull-fitted 'M7' No. 30129 waits at Yeovil Town, having brought in a shuttle service from the Junction. This locomotive was transferred away from Yeovil in March 1963, spending its last few months of service at Bournemouth from where it was withdrawn in November that year. *Jeffery Grayer*

Short-term steam replacements for the pensioned-off Drummond locomotives were mainly ex GW pannier tanks. Here an unidentified member of the class waits to leave Yeovil Junction with the connecting shuttle to Yeovil Town in 1964. In the distance, and coming towards the end of their reign on the Exeter route, a Bulleid Pacific is taking water at the east end of the up platform, both trains signalled away by semaphores situated on the gantry at the London end of the platform. The pannier with its Western Region coaches epitomises the takeover of motive power and stock by the SR's great rival in the West Country. Yeovil Junction shed had a number of panniers on its books from classes 57xx, 64xx and 54xx but their stay was to be short-lived on the shuttles, which were taken over by AC Cars railbuses in December 1964. The year before another change had taken place at Exeter, although less likely to have been noticed except by the enthusiast fraternity. This was the transfer from Exeter of the 'W' class 2-6-4T engines previously used to provide banking assistance up the incline from St Davids. They were replaced by the ubiquitous pannier tanks.

Warships ahoy!

Hence at the beginning of June, No. D829 *Magpie* arrived at Salisbury for crew training. Later in the month, D819 *Goliath* was provided for this duty and was in turn replaced by D824 *Highflyer* at the end of July. To simplify training only the Swindon-built 'Warships' were initially requested for the line, which excluded Nos. D800–802 (2,000hp engines), D818 (fitted with a different type of train-heat boiler) and D830 (having a Paxman engine). 'Hymeks' also penetrated the line with No. D7095 in operation on 6 June working ecs from Exeter to Clapham Yard in the early hours of Saturday morning, returning late that day with the Surbiton–Okehampton Car Carrier. Later in the year, classmate No. D7010 was employed on 24 October on a special from Yeovil to Waterloo.

Meanwhile, No. D829 made test runs to Waterloo on 9 August and it was expected that 17 August would see dieselisation introduced to the line, about thirty men having been trained on the Warships by this time. In fact, 17 August saw 'Warships' only on the 01.15, 13.00, and 19:00 down from Waterloo and the 07.30, 12.30 'ACE', and 17.54 trains up from Exeter. But even this was a welcome respite for the hard-pressed rostering staff as in the previous week 72A had been so short of motive power that two Pacifics had to be borrowed from Bournemouth shed, Nos

34053 *Sir Keith Park* and 35023 *Holland-Afrika Line*, together with the recently outshopped from Eastleigh, but not fully run in, No. 35007 *Aberdeen Commonwealth*, which was also commandeered to help out on the Exeter line.

On 11 June, 'Hymek' No. D7099 had charge of the returning Wadebridge–Kensington special carrying the Household Cavalry from the Royal Cornwall Show. Then on 30 July, (or 1 August, according to different sources), came the first reported working of a 'Warship' when No. D824 worked an express from Exeter to Salisbury returning on the Brighton–Plymouth train. From 17 August two more 'Warships' were allocated to 72A, one duty taking the 07.30 from Exeter to Waterloo returning at 13.00; followed by the 17.54 from Exeter returning with the 01.10 newspaper train from Waterloo. The second duty handled the 12.30 from Exeter, the 'ACE', returning with the 19.00 from Waterloo. During the first week, Nos. D815 *Druid*, D824 *Highflyer* and D827 *Kelly* were all noted in action on the 19.00 down service, although on the Saturday this had reverted to steam haulage with No. 35025 *Brocklebank Line*. Apparently during their turnround at Waterloo, the Warships were stabled in the Windsor line carriage sidings beyond platform 21. In the early part of August, a further shortage of available Pacifics also led to 'Standard Class 5s' putting in appearances.

Uneasy bedfellows. The new diesel traction often had to share space with steam – a practice that was far from ideal. Here 'Crompton' D6534 and Warship D829 *Magpie* share Salisbury shed with Standard 'Class 4' No. 76067 in the final year of Southern Region steam, 1967.

An interesting view showing three facets of the route at Sherborne now long gone. Most noticeable perhaps is the maroon-liveried 'Warship' getting away over the traditionally gated level crossing with a Waterloo service in the late 1960s. Also of note are the Royal Mail 'Morris 1000' vans delivering mailbags to the station for onward distribution – a scene now vanished forever from the railways. Lastly, on view is one of the modern signal boxes built in 1960 to replace original LSWR boxes. This lasted only until January 1970 when it, too, became redundant following replacement of the traditional gates by lifting barriers operated from a unit sited on the station platform.

A visit to Exmouth Junction shed on Sunday, 6 September, the day before official dieselisation, revealed that half the shed was reserved for diesel traction, while seen passing the shed that day was No. 34109 *Sir Trafford Leigh-Mallory* taking the last regular steam-hauled express into Exeter Central. The occasion of the final up steam-hauled 'ACE' had been on 14 August, with the last down steam-hauled service being on 4 September with a resplendent No. 35022 *Holland-America Line* in charge.

The new diesel-hauled, semi-fast timetable came into effect from Monday, 7 September 1964. However, hardly a day went by without steam turning up at Exeter, covering for a diesel failure with recourse being made again to borrowing Pacifics from Bournemouth-line trains. These frequent diesel failures, not just of locomotives but also of DMUs, were blamed by local railwaymen on the perception that the WR had provided 'clapped out' motive power for use on this now perceived secondary route, adding fuel to the deep-rooted suspicion that the WR was trying to kill off traffic on the line, leading to eventual closure of the route. To add insult to injury, the WR decided to introduce the alien concept of 'recovery time' to the new schedules, a practice previously unheard of between Salisbury and Exeter with the SR.

Overcrowding, particularly on Sundays when coach formations were reduced, became a constant complaint. Particular notice was focused on the former 'ACE' timing, the 11.00 from Waterloo, which now terminated at Salisbury feeding passengers for stations beyond into the Brighton–

Plymouth train. During the first week there were so many passengers for stations west of Salisbury carried by the 11.00 that the leading three-coach set from the 11.00 service had to be attached to the Brighton–Plymouth train, so making a fourteen-coach consist, a demanding task for a Warship on the switchback gradients of the Exeter line. The *Railway Observer* for December 1964 said that it was, 'Depressing to record little or no improvement in time keeping ... failures of the 'Warships' are all too frequent and the number of times that steam has replaced diesel traction are too frequent to record. The service is indeed a poor advertisement for modernisation.'

By the end of October, twenty-one different examples of 'Warships' had been noted at Waterloo, including the non-standard No. D830, the Paxman-engined locomotive. The sidings at Waterloo contained four 'Warships' on the morning of 9 October – Nos. D818 *Glory* and D828 *Magnificent* covering the 09.00 and 11.00 departures, together with D805 *Benbow* and D824 *Highflyer*, both of which had failed the previous day. The following day saw D823 *Hermes* and D831 *Monarch*, both serviceable, in company with non-runner D824 and a new failure in the shape of D813 *Diadem*. 'Hymeks' were also noted putting in appearances on West of England trains. Steam substitutes in this month included No. 34084 *253 Squadron* on the 10th and 18th, No. 35029 *Ellerman Lines* on the 24th, and No. 35030 *Elder Dempster Lines*, the latter also seen on the 10 October. No. 35030 achieved a twelve-minute gain on the diesel schedule between Yeovil Junction and Exeter Central with a maximum of 92mph recorded near Crewkerne.

A London-bound 'Warship' flashes over the deserted trackbed of the former S & D at Templecombe passing the now redundant LSWR water tower in the spring of 1968 with a mixture of green and blue/grey coaching stock.

A sad end for SR steam and where No. 34089 had been recorded earlier – Salisbury shed used as a dumping ground for withdrawn locomotives after July 1967. *Jeffery Grayer*

Nothing more powerful than 'Standard' tank No. 82030 was available to come to the rescue of a 'Warship' that had suffered an engine failure at Seaton Junction on 10 October. On Christmas Eve, No. D869 *Zest*, one of the final series of the class, was noted hauling the 11.00 departure from Waterloo, which was also extended beyond Salisbury to Exeter for the whole of the Christmas period. Other members of this final batch, namely Nos. D866 *Zebra*, D868 *Zephyr* and D870 *Zulu*, were seen regularly at Waterloo in the early months of 1965. In February, empty Meldon Quarry hopper trains were noted proceeding westwards behind 34006 *Bude* and 31791. On 5 March, No. 34015 *Exmouth* worked the 14.20 Exeter–Waterloo in place of a diesel and No. 35029 appeared on 3 March due to snow causing the late running of the incoming Warship-headed service. In 1965 the augmented Saturday service was not totally monopolised by 'Warships' as 'Cromptons' (Class 33) worked the 11.00 departure from Waterloo. Steam too appeared in the shape of No. 34013 *Okehampton* taking over the through train from Exmouth at Sidmouth Junction on 24 July and No. 34052 *Lord Dowding* heading the 16.30 from Exeter on 17 July.

Although all West of England services in the 1965 peak holiday season were rostered for diesel haulage, steam persisted on the 08.00 departure from Waterloo and the 11.15 and 14.13 through services from Exmouth. 'Type 2' locomotives of the D63xx Class generally handled the *branch* line portions of these services. With the non-availability of Salisbury and Exmouth Junction sheds for regular servicing, the Warships and rakes of coaching stock were serviced at Newton Abbot, resulting in 40 miles of non-revenue running to and from Exeter daily. At the Salisbury end, servicing had to be undertaken at Eastleigh, some 20 miles away, although crews continued to sign on at Salisbury and trains were berthed there. Later in 1967, Salisbury shed, along with Weymouth, was to become a dumping ground for redundant steam locomotives awaiting their final journeys to the scrapyards, a sombre sight as Warships on the mainline passed by the rusting grass-grown tracks of the former '72B'.

Diesel failures persisted into 1968 with nothing more than a three-car Hampshire DMU running from Salisbury in the path of the 11.10 from Waterloo on 7 November, which had failed at Andover. No. D806 *Cambrian*, the culprit, eventually arrived at Exeter 105 minutes down, piloted by 'Hymek' No. D7019. Members of (the original) Class 43 based at Laira also had on occasion to help out with Waterloo services. On 11 January 1969 the 09.10 from Waterloo was headed by D809 *Champion* but arrived at its destination sixty-three minutes late piloted by No. D7008. 'Western' class diesels also made the odd appearance; such as on 9 December 1970 when No. (D)1011 *Western Thunderer* worked the 18.05 Exeter–Waterloo instead of the usual Class 42. Much to the relief of the travelling public, the use of these unreliable 'Warship' diesel-hydraulics finished in October 1971 when they were replaced by the more reliable but less powerful 'Cromptons'. The last full day of 'Warship' operation was Saturday, 2 October 1971 when all six diagrams were Class 42 operated, with D808 *Champion* and D817 *Foxhound* both appearing in maroon livery with full yellow ends.

Powering up the grade from the now single-line Buckhorn Weston tunnel, a Waterloo service displaying headcode 62 is headed by a 'Crompton' hauling a rake of blue/grey Mark 1 stock.

Cromptons into the breach

As a consequence of their lower power rating, 1,550 bhp as against the nominal 2,200 bhp of the Warships, the schedules had to be eased when the 'Cromptons' took over. Passengers were no doubt pleased with the increased likelihood of reaching their destinations without a breakdown, however the increase in journey times was not a good marketing ploy.

Recourse to double-heading improved punctuality and this occurred regularly with the often heavily laden through Brighton service. A number of the Class 3 type had already been modified to work in push-pull mode with one or two '4-TC' units from Waterloo, as had happened with the Bournemouth electrification, and this at least reduced terminal time should a service arrive late. Meanwhile, in the 1970s the section between Wilton and Sherborne reverted back to SR control.

To a large part thanks to the perseverance of the Salisbury Area manager Gerald Daniels and following a seventeen-year hiatus, Templecombe station was reopened in 1983. It still has its art deco signal box, which latterly saw the dual role of ticket office. Here a 'Class 33' arrives with a down, Exeter-bound service. *Jeffery Grayer*

Another 'Crompton' rolls in to Whimple, illustrating well the use of the down platform, which unfortunately did not house the main station building. This was the disadvantage of singling with the existing facilities designed for separate 'up' and 'down' working, which did little to encourage passenger support. The other track occupying the up side was merely a siding to serve the remaining goods facility. The famous monkey puzzle tree, for so long a feature of this location, can be glimpsed on the far right. *Jeffery Grayer*

Power at last – the Class 50s

With the assistance of Class 31s on the more lightly loaded services, such as the 19.55 from Exeter to Basingstoke that seldom loaded beyond four coaches, the 'Cromptons' were the primary motive power for some nine years until improvements finally came with the cascading of the 2,700bhp Class 50s displaced in May 1980 from the Paddington route by IC 125s. Crew training began a few weeks previously, with No. 50050 *Fearless* being noted at Salisbury on 1 February with the 13.00 service from Waterloo, while on 12 February, No. 50007 *Hercules* was reported passing Basingstoke with the 09.00 from Waterloo to Exeter.

Class 50s, with No. 50015 *Valiant* nearest the camera, passing at Pinhoe where the double track from Exeter gives way to single. Although lifting barriers now adorn the level crossing, the old LSWR box (minus decorative valancing) remains *in situ* controlling movements at this location. No. 50015 saw service until 1990. Pinhoe was one of several places where trains might wait for a crossing movement. Arguably the most contentious of these was at Chard Junction. There, since closure of their station in 1966, local residents had been unable to access services, instead being compelled to make their way to either Axminster or Crewkerne. *Jeffery Grayer*

Illustrating one of the newer signal boxes, that opened in 1957, and this time showing a Class 50 paused 'wrong line' at Gillingham. This box would close in 2012, its functions being taken over by the new Basingstoke panel. *Jeffery Grayer*

The introduction of these more powerful locomotives resulted in a significant reduction in journey times of the order of thirty minutes in end to end timings, and still while retaining a similar number of stops. It had taken almost two decades but we were now back to finally matching the best steam times of twenty years earlier.

Failures still occurred, however, and when Class 33s were substituted, then naturally performance suffered. Indeed, during the period 1983–85 only some 65–70% of services were recorded as on time or less than five minutes late on arrival. Even so, there was no doubt the Class 50s were the best motive power that the line had enjoyed since the days of steam and their introduction together with the use of more modern Mark 2 coaching stock was perhaps a sign that the fortunes of this 'Cinderella' route were finally improving.

Last gasp of the loco-hauled services – the Class 47s

Although Class 47s had been used occasionally on the route back in the early 1970s when for example No. (D)1662 *Isambard Kingdom Brunel* was seen at the head of the 16.30 Exeter–Waterloo on 10 December 1970 and sister engine No. (D)1714 was noted working the 13.08 Waterloo–Exeter returning at 18.05 piloted by sister locomotive No. (D)1674

Samson on 19 January 1971, they did not fully come into their own until the 1980s. For example, in early April of 1971 the 07.45 Exeter–Waterloo had No. 47204 at its head and four days later No. 47094 worked the 17.55 Exeter–Waterloo. The Class 47 type assumed more of the workload than was originally first envisaged during the first fortnight of the new summer timetable when no fewer than fifteen failures of Class 50s occurred. No. 47078 *Sir Daniel Gooch* and Nos. 47436 and 47475 were all noted deputising for stricken Class 50s. Ultimately the performance of the Class 50s did improve and they continued to serve the route for some twelve years. By 1990, however, reliability of the Class 50s was becoming poor and despite an intensive maintenance programme instituted at Plymouth's Laira depot and a refurbishment programme carried out at Doncaster Works, it became increasingly obvious that they would have to be replaced. Consequently, 24 May 1992 saw the end of regular Class 50-hauled trains on the line, although the Class 47s that were cascaded in to replace them had previously been used in Scotland on the arduous 100mph Glasgow–Edinburgh push-pull services and were themselves therefore not in the finest condition.

Recourse to freight-only locomotives such as Railfreight 47s and civil engineers' Class 33s was frequent in the final months of locomotive-hauled services. The distinction of being the very last Class 50-hauled train to run on BR metals fell to a Waterloo–Exeter service that operated on 26 March 1994 behind Nos.

The final flowering of locomotive-hauled services on the route. The 12.17 Exeter–Waterloo service, smartly turned out in Network SouthEast livery (even if the concept of 'South-East was a bit lost in West Country Exeter) arriving at Salisbury in charge of No. 47709 on 22 March 1993. This was shortly before the introduction of the Class 159 DMUs. *Jeffery Grayer*

50050 and 50007 double-headed. More exotic motive power also visited the line in the shape of diverted WR IC 125 units that travelled this way when engineering work during 1980–81 blocked their normal route from Paddington to Exeter.

Diesel Multiple Units

DMUs played a major role in providing secondary services on the mainline and connecting branch line services until the majority were closed. They took over from steam on the following branch lines:

Lyme Regis – Dieselised from November 1963, worked by two-coach DMUs until single railcars took over from March 1965, continuing as such until closure. Steam made occasional returns covering for diesel failures, as witnessed on 3 October when 'Ivatt' No. 41295 put in an appearance.

Seaton – Introduced from 4 November 1963 and similarly just a single railcar saw out the final months before closure. In February 1965, due to a shortage of DMUs two 14xx tank engines, Nos. 1442 and 1450, were transferred from Yeovil shed to Exmouth Junction for this service, often operating the timetable as 'auto trains'.

Sidmouth – Dieselised in November 1963.

Exmouth – Dieselised in November 1963.

Yeovil Junction to Yeovil Town – Single-car railbuses were introduced in December 1964.

There were to be some lengthy journeys entrusted to DMUs with the introduction of the winter timetable in September 1964. Some local services from Salisbury ran through to Plymouth via Okehampton; to Ilfracombe and to Barnstaple Junction taking respectively a bone-shaking four hours forty minutes, four hours twenty-nine minutes, and three hours fifty-four minutes – quite a feat of endurance on a DMU that stopped at virtually every station en route, especially if you were in a car without toilet facilities.

Another feat of endurance that was foisted on customers occurred with the replacement of locomotive-hauled stock on the through Brighton–Exeter train by 'Hastings' DMUs. This occurred on the Saturdays' only diagram between 1972–1977 using a twelve-car train in summer and a six-car in winter, but at least always incorporating a buffet car unit. DMUs, were of course, to have a resurgence on the line from 1993 onwards when the Class 159s, and later converted Class 158s, became the mainstay of all services.

An Exeter-bound DMU waits almost sheepishly at Exmouth's platform No. 4, the sole remaining face after December 1968, at what was once the town's impressive four-platform terminus. All was subsequently swept away to make way for a relief road and replaced by a new single platform terminus built to cater for today's restricted clientele. Although once scheduled for closure, the Exmouth branch from Exeter survives and is the sole survivor of the SR's former Salisbury–Exeter branch lines. *Jeffery Grayer*

A busy mid-1960s view of Central station full of interest, illustrating the changeover from steam to diesel with steam still in evidence at the up platform, where the safety valves of an unidentified locomotive are lifting as a DMU leaves from the forward portion of the platform. Bay platform No. 4 sees passengers boarding green-liveried, loco-hauled carriage stock while a DMU waits in the down bay, platform No. 1, for Exmouth. At the main down platform, a further DMU can be seen. Note the Blue Circle cement hopper in the adjacent goods yard that, at this time, still retained its substantial goods shed.

The Presflo wagon in the yard on the right of this view of Exeter Central represents one of the few remaining freight flows on the route in the 1980s as Blue Circle Cement maintained a facility here. A Class 50 can be seen waiting at the up platform ready to depart for Waterloo. *Jeffery Grayer*

Freight

As mentioned in the earlier article in this series, freight was deliberately removed from the route in order to give priority to passenger services operating over the long sections of single line. One of the few remaining freight workings was the MWFO dedicated coal distribution train from Didcot that, hauled by a Class 37, served the domestic coal depots at Yeovil Junction and at Exmouth Junction until 1991. The Shellstar fertiliser depot at Gillingham, milk depots at Chard Junction and Seaton Junction, Blue Circle cement at Exeter Central all continued to be served for some years during our period of review, with Class 47s from Crewe generally handling the fertiliser traffic. After withdrawal of the Yeovil Junction service, coal continued to be delivered to Exmouth Junction but now from Usk running via Taunton and Exeter Riverside, whence a Class 08 usually tripped the wagons up to Exmouth Junction. A Class 50 or Class 47 performed banking duties up the incline to Central station, a feature that had been missing from the scene for several years. Class 33s on Meldon ballast workings have already been touched upon, these often running at night when passenger traffic was lighter. Cider products from Whimple, until production ceased in 1989, and milk from Chard Junction often had Type 2 diesel motive power, trips being initially worked by Class 22s but later superseded by Laira-based Class 25s. D63xx locos based at Yeovil shed for banking on the Weymouth line made forays into the Yeovil area generally on ballast workings. Class 31s also appeared on the 19.35 Exeter–Basingstoke and 06.45 Salisbury–Exeter mixed workings, which included parcels vans, especially if the normally rostered Class 33 had been purloined for a Meldon ballast working. All in all, quite a variety of diesel power could be seen on the few remaining freight turns on the routes

Hopes for the future

Rebranding, within the new Network Southeast structure, which had been established in 1986, gave rise to improvements resulting from having a unified management structure rather than the division of the Salisbury–Exeter line between two regions. Repainting of locomotives, stock and stations were just the external visible signs of a more dynamic management approach under the lead of the redoubtable Chris Green in which proactive marketing strategies were developed to attract more customers. The final improvement came in 1993 with the concept of 'Total Route Modernisation', which saw an end to the long tradition of using cascaded second-hand locomotives and stock rendered surplus elsewhere on the network. For the first time since the 1950s new rolling stock, in the shape of the Class 159 DMUs introduced at a cost of £33million, was allocated to the line with their own newly constructed and dedicated Traincare Depot at Salisbury.

One of the mainstays of freight traffic during the line's heyday was milk and here we see a yellow-liveried diesel shunter, used to shunt wagons inside the United Dairies' creamery compound, parked on one of the sidings at Chard Junction. Milk traffic was lost by rail in 1980 and today the creamery, which had been established here in the 1930s by United Dairies, has been razed to the ground. The now demolished up side buildings of the closed Chard Junction station can be seen in the left background. *Jeffery Grayer*

A reminder of the glory days – the privately sponsored 'Blackmore Vale Express' headed by No. 35028 *Clan Line* enters Sherborne in October 1986, more than twenty years after regular steam services on the line came to an end. *Jeffery Grayer*

The final Class 47-operated service ran on 11 July 1993 and so brings us to the end of our thirty-year review of motive power that has seen the route relegated to secondary status, largely singled, operated with inferior, often worn-out, stock and locomotives only to rise again towards the end of the twentieth century into something approaching mainline status once more. Rising passenger demand in the twenty-first century will hopefully continue to be a stimulus for further improvements, thereby ensuring the line's long-term future. But its very survival was at one time 'a damned nice thing – the nearest run thing you ever saw in your life', to correctly quote the oft misquoted remark of the Duke of Wellington after that other battle of Waterloo!

Appendix 1: Through coaches

Examination of the last summer timetable under the old regime, 15 June–6 September 1964, reveals the following provision of through coach services –

From Waterloo		Serving
Mondays–Fridays		
01.10		TC Ilfracombe and Plymouth
09.00		TC Plymouth and Barnstaple Junction
11.00	ACE	TC Ilfracombe and Padstow *
11.05	ACE	TC Padstow +
13.00		TC Plymouth
Saturdays		
00.45		TC Ilfracombe, Torrington, Padstow and Bude
08.03		TC Exmouth and Sidmouth
08.35		TC Ilfracombe and Plymouth
09.00		TC Sidmouth and Exmouth
10.35	ACE	TC Padstow and Bude
11.00	ACE	TC Ilfracombe and Torrington
11.15		TC Padstow and Bude
11.45		TC Ilfracombe
13.00		TC Plymouth and Ilfracombe
15.00		TC Plymouth and Ilfracombe

*Until 24 July and from 21 August, also Fridays only
31 July, 7 and 14 August
+Mondays–Thursdays 27 July–20 August

The summer of 1963 had seen the final through coaches from Waterloo to Lyme Regis and to Seaton. After 1963 through coaches to Sidmouth and Exmouth via Tipton St Johns continued to run on Saturdays only in the summers of 1964 and 1965.

The only remaining through service was the Brighton–Plymouth, which operated as far as Plymouth until March 1967, when it was cut back to Exeter. Even this Exeter remnant was withdrawn in 1971, although partially reinstated the following summer.

In 1982 the service was extended to Paignton for the summer months and the following year a through service to Penzance was introduced on Fridays with a Saturday service to Plymouth via Newton Abbot extended to Penzance in the summer.

The year 1964 was to be the final season of the Surbiton–Okehampton Car Carrier train, which had been introduced in 1960. The final run was in September 1964, so outlasting the 'ACE' by just one week.

Appendix 2: Steam power

Pacific motive power based at Exmouth Junction in 1963
(Recoded 83D in 9/63 – Closed to steam 6/65 – used for stabling diesels until ?/67)

No.	Allocation Ended	No.	Allocation Ended
34002	8/64	34065	3/64
34011	11/63	34066	8/64
34015	8/64	34069	11/63
34020	9/64	34070	8/64
34023	8/64	34072	7/64
34024	10/63	34074	5/63
34030	9/64	34096	9/64
34032	10/63	34106	9/64
34033	8/64	34107	9/64
34035	5/63	34108	10/63
34036	10/63	34109	9/64
34054	from 10/63 until 9/64	34110	11/63
		35003	6/64
34056	10/63	35009	9/64
34058	10/63	35010	8/64
34060	10/63	35013	8/64
34061	from 10/63 until 7/64	35022	2/64
		35025	9/64
34062	7/64	35026	2/64
34063	5/63		

A Visit to Feltham Shed
Summer 1964

Les Price

It was a warm and clear June evening and I had recently moved into a hostel at Sunbury-on-Thames, just 3 miles down the road from Feltham Motive Power Depot. A fellow train enthusiast and I decided to cycle there after work. Neither of us, a Somerset lad and a Salopian, had previously seen any Southern freight locomotives so the closeness of the shed was too good a chance to miss.

A brief look into history may be appropriate. By 1910, the pressure of freight traffic coming into London from the South-West had begun to overwhelm the existing facilities at Nine Elms and consequently the LSWR sought what was then a green-field site. In 1921 Feltham was developed as a modern 'Hump' Marshalling Yard, and the loco shed was built at the same time. The age of freight concentration had begun and the yard would soon became the busiest in the country.

Forty years later on that day in 1964, the shed foreman agreed we could take a look around and it was a melancholy site; the number of stored locomotives almost matched those in service. Rusting engines sat on rusting rails at the front of the shed: they included a Bulleid 'Austerity' 'Q1' Class 0-6-0 No. 33010, in front of which was a Maunsell 'W' Class 2-6-4T No. 31912 and alongside which was a Urie-designed 'S15' Class 4-6-0 No. 30499.

The 'Q1' had been in store since September 1963 and looked in poor condition. By contrast, No. 31912 was at rest,

still in light steam, probably after shunting duties in the yard. Designed by Maunsell, she was newly out-shopped from Eastleigh in 1932 but had only another three months of active life left; she was withdrawn at the end of August 1964.

On the other hand, the 'S15' No. 30499 had fared and would fare slightly better. Despite her rusting wheels, at the end of 1963 she had her original Urie double bogie 5,000 gallon tender replaced by an Ashford 4,000 gallon tender. But a short time later, on 5 January 1964, she too had been taken out of service.

However, No. 30499 had something of a 'Cinderella' aura about her. The Urie Society website notes she was sold to Messrs Woodhams for scrap shortly after the photograph was taken. Thereafter, she was at Barry for sixteen years; during which time she lost her tender for a second time.

In the meantime the Urie Society had purchased her sister engine, No. 30506, and transported her to the Mid-Hants Railway for restoration. Then in 1980, No. 30499 was bought, originally with the intention of using her as a full set of spares for No. 30506. Since then, a rethink had taken place, and another Maunsell double bogie 5,000 gallon tender was bought from Barry in order that she might be restored in her own right. As I write, No. 30499 is at Ropley in the course of a painstaking full restoration. Perhaps after the whims of circumstance, No. 30499 will, eventually, get to the ball!

Evening time at Feltham MPD and a number of stream locos await their fate. Alongside the 'Crompton' is 'Q1' No. 33010, withdrawn since 14 September 1963 and with rust covering its wheels. In front is 'W' No. 31912, it would survive for just three months more. To the right is one of the original LSWR 'S15' 4-6-0s introduced in 1920. This loco, withdrawn on 5 January 1920, had been a long-term Feltham resident. A further unidentified withdrawn 'S15' stands on the extreme right. *Les Price*

Inside Feltham shed, the crew of No. 30842 give the locomotive their attention prior to leaving the shed to work for a night freight to Salisbury. *Les Price*

Three of the few active locomotives were inside the shed. One was another 'S15' 4-6-0 No. 30823, introduced by Maunsell and built at Eastleigh in March 1927 with modifications to Urie's original design. Then there was BR 'Standard Class 5' 4-6-0 No. 73084, once named *Tintagel*, and BR 'Standard Class 4' 2-6-4T No. 80095, overall a real mix of ancient and modern.

Meanwhile, out in the yard, locomotives were being prepared for their night's work. The 'S15' 4-6-0 No. 30842, another we had seen inside the shed earlier, was now moving forward to take on water before working a night freight to Salisbury.

Another Bulleid 'Austerity' Q1 0-6-0, No. 33012, was sitting outside the shed, the fireman busy performing his final checks. She also then moved off to take on water, silhouetted as the sun set in the west behind her. She was rostered to carry out an interesting working. With a home crew, the engine was due off shed at 10.27 pm to work the 10.45 pm freight from Feltham Yard to Wimbledon West Yard where she was due at 12.40 am. From 12.45 am until 1.15 am her task was to shunt the yard there. At 1.30 am she was booked to run light engine through to Clapham Junction via East Putney and Mount Pleasant Junction, due there at 1.48 am. At Clapham, Nine Elms men relieved the Feltham crew. They then worked the 2.30 am milk tanks train forward to the Express Dairies Depot at Morden. These tanks had been part of a second milk train that ran up daily from Torrington.

So we cycled back to Sunbury in the slowly fading light that follows the sunset on a summer evening. And just as surely, the sun was setting on the future of Feltham Shed and its yard. The shed closed in 1967 and with the persistent decline in rail-borne freight traffic, Feltham Yard itself followed on 6 January 1969. The site is now occupied by the Jubilee Mail Centre, a giant Royal Mail sorting office that handles mail for most of South-West London and Surrey.

On the same evening, 'Q1' No. 33012 received its final checks from the fireman before her own night's duty as described in the text. *Les Price*

Rebuilt
The Letters and Comments Pages

We start this issue's selection with one from **Alan Blackburn reference the 'Portsmouth Direct' in** *SW44.*

'Having lived and worked on the Portsmouth Direct line all my life I found Jeremy Clarke's article most interesting. That Thomas Brassey built the line as a speculative venture is quite well known, what is perhaps less well known is that at the same time he was building the Direct line he was also constructing the Wimbledon to Epsom route and the Yeovil to Exeter railway. Not a man to waste money he used the drawings for the station buildings at Liphook, Liss and Rowlands Castle for Worcester Park and Ewell, whilst those for Godalming and Petersfield were used for Crewkerne, Axminster, Honiton, Sidmouth (Junc), Whimple and Broad Clyst. I do not think that any were exact copies but the inspiration is clearly there.

'Mention has been made at different times and in several places of the fact that the 4-COR/RES and BUF were underpowered in comparison with the earlier Brighton line stock and indeed the 2-BILs. Well, in theory they may have been, but I doubt any of the earlier stock ever ran faster. A 'Pompey' at speed was truly a sight to behold. The Portsmouth men were used to fast running and the time keeping in the 1950s was impeccable – God help the Signalman who delayed one! Things were helped by the Official Notice in Havant Box to the effect that under no circumstance was a London West train to be delayed by a Central one – old loyalties it seemed die hard! One train though that never ran to time was the

One that was omitted, purely for space reasons, from Terry Cole's recent 'Special Issue' on steam around Brighton, was this of 'E4' No. 32480 near to Eridge with a train for Lewes and Brighton on 12 March 1952 formed of a three-coach coach 'Birdcage' set, which also had two cattle vans at the rear.

'fourth fast' of the hour on summer Saturdays. This was made up of whatever was available from BILs to SUBs. It was said that the number of 'Jumper' cables made them sluggish.

That the Pompey stock could run very fast there was no doubt. One Sunday evening in the early fifties I was on duty at Fratton West as the 'box boy' (Signal Lad) when a empty special was arranged by 'Control' to run from Fratton to Durnsford Road. I gave Control the departure time as the unit cab passed the box and thought no more about it. About an hour later Control rank up querying the departure time I had given them. We compared our clock times and it seemed this empty train had arrived at Wimbledon in some quite unbelievable time that averaged more than 70mph. Obviously the Driver wanted an early finish … . Happy days.

Still on the subject of the **Portsmouth Direct,** but this on the **mystery image** that was shown on **p.66 of *SW45*. From Colin Martin**: 'No mystery to me and no, that is not me with Mum & Dad either! It's Milford, Surrey.

'Sometimes a simple view can trigger the memory, and back when the world was young, and black and white, a five minute bike ride after tea gave me many a misspent evening at Milford and its environs awaiting the passage of the 6.45 pm pick-up goods. This was usually a 'U' class 2-6-0 with maybe only a half a dozen vans, but I can also recall a 'King Arthur' and a 'Q1' on the same working. There was also another pick up at 8.45 pm, both of these stopped at Farncombe West box and then reversed into Godalming Old Station, which was goods only until closure in the '70s.

'I recognised the houses in the background straightaway, but still some doubt remained, so a trip back to the station immediately dispelled any doubt, (your pic is on the up side).'

The rarely recorded signal box at Meldon Junction south of Okehampton, where the single line diverged to Halwill. *Robert Iredale*

Now from **Michael Upton** on the **signalling** aspects of the currently running series on the **Salisbury–Exeter'** line.

'This is indeed a rich seam of a topic, and I will endeavour to find out what my colleague remembers about the Salisbury–

Exeter singling. He is, I suspect, one of the few people still around who actually worked on the project, being at the time a signalling designer. I don't recall any mention before of the use of EKT (Electric Key Token), but it was the WR preferred option for single lines. However, the avoidance of the need to deliver tokens, meaning the train would not have to come to a stand at the SB, was and still is one of the advantages of Tokenless Block (TB), and with no stations at Wilton, Templecombe (at that time), Chard and Pinhoe that may have been deemed too restrictive if EKT was to be used.

As a point of interest, we in the Network Rail Reading Signalling Design office have recently issued a design for a new WR Tokenless Block (TB) system (the same as the Salisbury–Exeter system) to replace GWR Lock and Block (L&B) between Malvern Wells and Ledbury. The L&B is now unique and spares are impossible to source – the L&B instruments have been reserved by the NRM, with the work to be carried out soon.

I do know the SR did not like EKT, preferring Tablets, but I do not know why, I will ask around; someone must know, or at least have an opinion. It is said that if you get three signal engineers in a room you will get four opinions!

There has been some work carried out by us to see how the EKT from Yeovil Pen Mill to Maiden Newton might be replaced with something else. It is difficult to keep up staff competence for that line and also Marchwood (which is, I think, as good as mothballed now).

We have two of the Salisbury–Exeter TB instruments in our office for safe keeping, another two will be used on the Malvern Wells–Ledbury project. I will gather the details regarding their conversion and send to you. As far as I can remember, the commutator was changed to show 'NORMAL' or 'ACCEPT and OFFER' and 'TRAIN ARRIVED COMPLETE' plungers added. Probably only the case and the indicator were common but the WR was frugal when it came to signalling, and if it saved a few quid they would do it.

I do know a bit about TB – well, the WR one, anyway – there is a Scottish version and a BR version, also an Isle of Wight system unique to that line, the difference being the signaller does not need to operate a Train Arrived Complete control. So if you have any questions about the WR TB I will be pleased to try and assist.

Back to the EKT on Salisbury–Exeter, I think it unlikely the WR would have requested the return of the EKT instruments because at that time significant numbers must have been (or were shortly going to be) made redundant by wholesale line closures – just a thought. So perhaps the SR did have plans to use them.'

Following an email response from the office, a second letter was received from Michael that commented upon some of my own notes. I am sure the reader will have no difficulty in picking up on the points mentioned.

'You are correct regarding the Lock and Block instruments and the jobbing shop when it was at Woodley for a short time – I still sometimes see Neil Milton, the manager at that time, ex-Ashford works apprentice.

'I would be happy to provide some help for the Salisbury–Exeter signalling, in fact I spoke to my colleague today who was one of the designers, and he has promised some info when he has a chance to recall the project. I will send to you if you are interested as I asked if he would be good enough to write it down.

'I too have always been more interested in the operational aspect of the railways rather than just the locomotives, but I too cannot resist a Bulleid!

'I will have a look to see if I can locate some wiring design to show the operation of TB. There are a number of write-ups on the internet (I cannot vouch for their accuracy), but I know somewhere I have a description of the system as first proposed before a test rig was set up in the Reading Signal Works to prove the system. This rig identified a number of problems, one of which was the difficulty in reliably proving a train entering the single line section for the purposes of standing behind the home signal to go back towards the box, with a train in the section going away towards the next SB, for instance as a run round. This is still allowed on the Scottish TB but a special 'token' is needed. On the WR system it was decided that by the time it was implemented those kind of moves would be rare and if needed a full single line release requiring the whole section clear would suffice.

'I liked your description of working Northam, an article about illicit SB visits might be interesting, there are lots of stories out there to be told I am sure!'

From **Tony Bloomfield** reference **Honor Oak Park – p.41, SW45**. 'I hope I'm sending this to the right place.' *(As you gather Tony – absolutely!)* 'I don't believe the bottom picture on page 41 of *SW45* is actually at Honor Oak Park. Memory, possibly faulty, says that the station buildings at HOP were on the overbridge on the road of the same name at the south end of the platforms. Also, the next station north is Brockley, and, at least in the 1950s, the line was four-track. The station south of Nunhead, on the old Crystal Palace HL line was just called Honor Oak, i.e. without the Park, And I always found it strange that 'honour' is spelt in the 'colonial' fashion … .'

And on a **similar tack from John Keane**, 'I have just been enjoying reading yet another very interesting issue (No. 45) of *Southern Way*. I'm writing regarding a small but important caption correction to the photo at the bottom of p.41 in the Southern Civil Engineering photo-spread. The station pictured with the new platform extension is Honor Oak on the Crystal Palace High Level branch, and not Honor Oak Park station, over the hill, on the London Bridge–Brighton main line. The sidings bottom right of the picture are the station's three-road coal siding adjacent to Wood Vale.'

From **Pawel Nowak** on various topics in **SW45**. Thank you for assembling the excellent range of historic material in *Southern Way* and its associated special issues, *(We try but it is certainly not all me. Most of the contributions are from readers, some*

With thanks to Bryan Simmonds.

old hand, some recent. All are welcome and we do try and use them all. Only once has something appeared under a pseudonym and for very good reason – and that did not originate from me either. If you do wish your name to be withheld in correspondence do please tell us.).

'Some of the articles in the latest edition pose questions to which I will tentatively attempt some answers.

Southern Civil Engineering, p.40: 'These Slade Green photos will be views of the 1926-built Repair Shop on a site south-east of the original steam locomotive shed. Originally it was equipped to lift and overhaul coaches in the prevailing two and three-car formations, but a later eastern extension had to be built to handle four-car units when suburban eight-car formations went from 3+2+3 to 4+4 by expanding the former three-car motored sets by an additional coach and withdrawing the two-car trailer sets, which were previously sandwiched between them for rush-hour use. One of these trailer sets can be seen in the top right photograph. The earlier double-ended steam loco shed was intended for an allocation of up to 100 (fairly short) locomotives for suburban passenger and freight workings and well over 700ft long, so more than adequate for stabling eight eight-car electric formations. The brick walls and entrances were retained and the roof remodelled by removal of the rows of chimneys and associated troughs

within the structure, to be replaced by a 'trolley-jumper' system to supply current to units standing within the shed, which had no third-rail provision inside for obvious safety reasons and where inspection pits were in use. In the 1950s, the ten-car scheme required a brick-walled extension to the existing structure at the London end.' (See also *An Illustrated History of Slade Green Depot* by A,W. Deller, Irwell Press, 1994).

P.41: 'The impedance bond as shown in the top photo was a favourite target for copper thieves, and hence a major source of signalling and traction power failure. The interesting second feature in the photograph is the fourth rail fixed to the sleepers off-centre in the 'four-foot' space between the running rails. This feature, also visible at Sundridge Park (p.42), assisted with providing a good return current path on single-ended branches. As the mystery location was obviously rural at the time but worth electrifying for future traffic, this suggests somewhere like Eden Park on the Hayes branch or perhaps somewhere on the Tattenham Corner line. Incidentally, the ex-LCDR station in the photo at the bottom of p.41 was known as plain 'Honor Oak' in the last years of its existence in the 1950s, with the Honor Oak Park name applicable to the surviving station south of Brockley on the nearby Brighton Main Line. As both were adjacent to the park, did the original builders of the line to Crystal Palace HL also use 'Park' in the name?'

The advantage of Rebuilt is that is does give the opportunity for 'odd' images to be included and so gain a wider audience, which might otherwise remain hidden away. Agreed, not the best quality, but we have the late Mr Drummond's 'Bug' at Southampton Docks during the time it was used to ferry visitors around the complex – often spoken of but never, as far as we know – ever photographed other than at Eastleigh.

The EPB Story, Part 7, p.51: 'I don't know whether David Monk-Steel intends to continue the story beyond 1969 *(we do hope so. Ed.),* but in case not, it is worth noting that growth of summer passenger traffic to Folkestone Harbour and Dover Marine and the use of MLVs in pairs on many trains led to a shortage of mail/parcels/luggage accommodation. A batch of BR standard 'BG' passenger-rated full-brake vans was adapted as 'Trailer Luggage Vans' with jumper cables and duplicated air pipes suitable for use between an MLV and the adjacent CEP driving motor coach. This ingenious idea was very short-lived as drivers objected to using them on the non-electrified dockside lines for which they were intended on grounds of the lack of visibility when propelling from the driving cab in areas open to dock workers, seamen, etc. For a few years, these vehicles ended up working Christmas season mail and parcels trains sandwiched between two MLVs, in the manner of other parcels stock as described in the article.'

P.66: 'With regard to the question in Nicholas Owen's letter about the unusual platform arrangement at Victoria (Central Division), in my schooldays I was always struck by how long the platforms were when leaving in a 4-LAV or a 2-HAL/2-BIL formation for stations on the Brighton Main Line. Each pair of the relevant platforms was nearly twenty coaches long and the points and signals in the middle permitted an eight-car train 'on the buffers' to leave the station while another eight-car train was standing at the 'country' or south end of the same platform through the additional line. This permitted the station to handle many more trains in the available width without overflowing on to Buckingham Palace Road! The growing number of peak-hour twelve-car formations restricted the usefulness of this facility and the desire to redevelop the 'air-space' over the platforms and enlarge the cramped station concourse led to removal of this ingenious layout.

I can't think of an exact duplicate of the Victoria arrangement, as the middle lines between each pair of platforms at Manchester Central were just for locomotive release and possibly some stabling. In the wider railway, mid-platform crossover connections are quite common where it is still useful to operate two parts of a long platform independently. Surviving examples include Bournemouth, York, Cambridge, Edinburgh Waverley and (on a smaller scale), Doncaster Platform 3 and Sheffield Platform 1. What has mostly disappeared, though, is the large number of scissors crossovers and 'middle lines' in the space between the platform lines, Exeter Central being a major Southern Railway example. These crossovers (and the separate 'middle boxes' that worked them in Absolute Block semaphore days) were essential for attaching portions when working locomotive-hauled passenger trains in order to release the incoming locomotive of the rear portion. The two portions were attached either by reversing the front portion using the through train locomotive or preferably using a 'station pilot' locomotive to push the rear coaches forward.'

Now from **Jeremy Clark** re *SW45* EPB Part 7. 'The heading photo is taken on the now-four track section of the Kent Coast line between Rainham and Newington.'

From **Antony Hemens, *SW45***. 'On p.12 of the above edition there is a view of 'I3' Class No. 2082 near Chichester. I have further details that might be of interest to readers as follows: it is passing Bartholomews' *Sidings (where horse feed was also sold to the public – Ed.)* Between the wars, the level crossing (distance) was replaced by a single-carriageway bridge for the Chichester bypass and on 14 September 1944 eventually carrying a dual carriageway. The signal box also gave way to a ground frame.

'Bartholomews' carried imported grains/seeds, used in the production of animal feedstuffs and also produced fertilisers. When seen in 1970, by the gate to the sidings on the up line there was signal gantry with home and distance signals. On the other

No we have not gone 'all LNER', but Steve Banks – a renowned authority on LNER carriage workings – asks the question why would a single GN brake be attached to what is clearly a rake of otherwise SR vehicles on this through train at Banbury? The only other information we have is that it dates from 1951. Suggestions would be welcome. So far all we can come up with is that the SR brake vehicle developed a fault and this was the replacement.

side facing inside the gate was a stop signal. These were both rail built. The sidings were still in existence until 14 November 1987 with Rail Freight covered wagons in the yard, but by then the mechanical signals had been removed.'

Now from **Colin Duff re SCT in *SW45*,** 'Regarding the lost archives of Stephen Townroe Part 10, p.78, the upper picture with the BSA motorbike. Although this is on the eastern approach to Esher station I reckon it is the (A309) Hampton Court Way at Weston Green, Thames Ditton. The houses seen under the arch in the distance beyond the right-hand retaining wall I used to run past during cross-country in school games lessons. The cross-country circuit then took a turn along a footpath parallel to the embankment (the other side of the embankment in the picture) and from there I used to delight in watching the final days of steam and the intriguing electric lash-ups in use leading up to full electric workings to Bournemouth. So much so that the delay due to my train-watching threatened to make me late back to school and miss the school bus home. On the positive side, my resultant running time was so slow it meant I was never selected for the school team, which suited me very well. I can also just make out, on the left, the location of the 'Lamb and Flag' pub, one of my granddad's haunts.

Sadly away from thoughts of a drink in the pub mentioned above, this is from **John Raggett re *SW44* and Peasmarsh Junction.** 'As always, a fascinating read. The photo on p.19 shows the formation leading from Peasmarsh Junction towards the river. What it doesn't show is a brick arch, hidden by the roof of the railway cottages in the right foreground. This was constructed to carry the line over a footpath, the line of which follows the hedgerow across the photo from the footbridge over the main line, these days an SR type prefabricated concrete structure. The brick arch used to be visible from the train, somewhat derelict and vandalised. The track bed of the Guildford to Horsham railway now forms part of the Downs Link leisure way – I took a spin on my bike last summer from Cranleigh to Guildford following this link. The footpath/cycleway leads right up to the location of Peasmarsh Junction and continues back to the river following the formation shown in the photo. I was surprised to find that not only is the brick arch still there, it has at sometime in the recent past, been restored including underpinning of the piers with concrete. The embankment ends abruptly at the river, extreme caution being needed descending to the tow path, especially on a bike! A wartime pillbox was sited here. The whole route is now completely enclosed by trees and few people these days will be aware of it. A couple of photos attached may be of interest.

> THE NATIONAL TRUST
> RIVER WEY NAVIGATIONS
>
> THIS WORLD WAR II PILL BOX WAS ONE OF OVER 5,000 BUILT IN THE EARLY 1940s. IT FORMED PART OF THE INLAND GHQ DEFENCE LINE. THIS WAS THE LAST OF A NUMBER OF DEFENCE LINES PROTECTING THE CAPITAL AND KEY INDUSTRIAL AREAS. THIS LINE EXTENDED FROM THE WEST COAST NEAR BRISTOL OVER TO THE KENT COAST NEAR CHATHAM.
> PILL BOX POSITIONS TOOK ADVANTAGE OF NATURAL AND MAN-MADE OBSTACLES SUCH AS RIVERS, CANALS AND EMBANKMENTS AND HOUSED MACHINE GUN AND ANTI-TANK WEAPONS.

Surviving railway arch. This is one still maintained by Network Rail.

Pillbox by the river (and John Raggett's bike!).

'The unreported location of the 'Bournemouth Belle' at the top of p.44 is Woking Junction. I particularly like the photo at the bottom of the same page as it shows in the left background an Aldershot and District Dennis bus parked up opposite the Odeon and behind it a double-decker London Transport STL type, one of a handful built with low-height bodies (most had 'highbridge' bodies), some of which were allocated to country routes that encountered low bridges.'

Now from **Wayne Thompson** on the subject of **Eastleigh in *SW45***. 'First of all I must say I always look forward to every issue of *Southern Way* and the specials, of which I have every one. I have been meaning to drop you an e-mail for a while and I suppose many ask you for articles of so-and-so, etc. But an article on Lancing works got me thinking (reading back issues!).

'I have worked on the footplate at Eastleigh for over forty-one years, bar a three-year gap at Fratton, yet I know virtually nothing about Eastleigh carriage works. Is there any merit in an article about the works, such as layout, or in a similar vein to the Lancing article? I have seen very few pictures of the site and yet it is very familiar to me virtually every working day, as many of the buildings still stand. Just a thought!' *(Wayne – thank you. Genuinely we would love to include an article on the Carriage Works at Eastleigh but the short answer is we just do not have the material and I regret nothing pending either. What odd images have surfaced we have included in past*

Right: **Wayne Thompson in his accompanying letter asks about an article on the carriage works. I really wish we could, but until such times ... the motor coach of a '4-COR' receives attention with a BR Mk1 behind.**

Below: **Southern Railway Carriage & Wagon Works, Eastleigh 1937. Surely this would not just have been staff engaged at the actual sawmill?**

issues of SW *in the hope of drawing out more, but so far to no avail. It just goes to show how some topics just seem to be blank. So, and I am sure not just for Wayne's sake, if anyone does have some suitable material please let us know – Ed.)*

Wayne continues, 'Anyway to the main reason for the e-mail. Most of the South Western side is well known to me and I love looking at the photographs from long ago of places I know so well. The Stephen Townroe pictures on p.87 and 88 got me thinking. At first I took the photo on p.87 at face value, although I couldn't place the location. But then the upper picture on p.88 made me doubt the first picture's location. I would say both are taken on the same trip, but there isn't anywhere on the line to Salisbury from Eastleigh that resembles the second picture. However, I now think I know where it could be. I suspect the trip was from Eastleigh towards Fareham. The second picture looks very much like the reverse bend on the down line about a mile from, and on the approach to, Botley. The lie of the land certainly is the same, the Botley to Bishops Waltham branch would be hugging the hillside of the trees beyond the chimney and Botley village would be off to the right. So, to the first picture. I think it was taken slightly earlier in the trip, shortly after leaving Eastleigh. At first I wasn't sure, but I think it is about half a mile after passing Eastleigh South Junction. This would be on the embankment over the Itchen Valley with Allington Lane bridge in the background. The doubt was that I couldn't see the bridge over the River Itchen, but I think the loco has probably just passed over it. Again the lay of the surrounding land is similar, as I am struggling to place a similar location on the line to Salisbury. But I could be wrong! Particularly if it were two separate trips!'

We have also received two letters from **Eric Youlden** re *SW45*.

First of all in the recent article on Billinton, Mr Youlden comments that the author omits to mention that when speaking of the 'B4X' class the use of a 'K' class boiler is not mentioned.

Now on to 'Salisbury – Exeter'. 'The author describes the 'Devon Belle' as being 'notionally' non-stop Waterloo to Exeter. Don't you believe it! It always, in both directions, called at Sidmouth Junction. What's more, for its final season in 1954, the down 'Belle' operated to a somewhat different schedule on Fridays. Waterloo departure was at 4.40 pm and the train called this time at Salisbury for an engine change, Axminster and then Sidmouth Junction on its way to Exeter Central.'

We regret that purely for reasons of space, further correspondence has been held over to the next issue – Ed.

The saga of No. 35004 rumbles on. This is a find by Ian Shawyer showing the engine in its final resting place and separated from its tender. The scrappers would attend to her where she stood. BUT my memory is not deceiving me as I had also been convinced I had seen the FNS tyre had broken in the slip – and here indeed is proof.

Pulverised Fuel Part 2
No. A629

The only additional English view within the German article was this (retouched view) of A629 at Ashford in 1930.

A 'certain' type of law transpired, literally just as *SW46* was all buttoned up and ready to go. This was the appearance of a further article, this time located in the German Magazine *Eisenbahn Kurier Special 7*, which is a first-hand account from the German engineer involved in the A629 experiments.

The piece, written in German, affords a most interesting, and mainly first-hand account of the trials. We are most grateful to our good friend Gerry Nichols of the Stephenson Locomotive Society for first of all locating the piece and also for the English translation. (The piece is reproduced without correction and in places shows the interesting way German interpretation was made of our railway system – and our language!)

The article commences with a description and comments on similar experiments in Germany, after which the author continues:

After, the author was commissioned to equip a 2-6-0 mixed traffic locomotive of class 'U', company number A629, in the railway workshops of Ashford (Kent) with an AEG coal-dust fire and also to erect a coal-dust grinder plant in Eastbourne engine shed. Thus, the AEG, through its commissioner, had some influence on the nature of the coal dust, especially since, in contrast to the experiments in Hennigsdorf, a highly active coal from the Dalton Main area (Rotherham) was to be used.

The Southern Railway had a specific traffic problem, which it was believed to be best solved by charcoal dust-fired locomotives. It had a train connection from London to Brighton with non-stop trains, which the businessmen of the City of London were to use to reach their families on the south coast of Britain in the shortest possible time at the weekend. Since the land rises to the south of London, the overcoming of which places particularly high demands on the work of the boiler without increasing driving time, the coal-dust firing that is related to load seemed to be particularly suitable for this. It was therefore to be expected that the lessons learned in Hennigsdorf would produce positive results.

The Dalton Main coal provided had a calorific value of 7,800 kcal/kg at a grade of about 40% volatile components and about 5% ash. This fuel also initially encountered difficulties, which required, above all, an in-depth trial of the suction train system as well as an empirical co-ordination of primary and secondary air. It turned out that the amount of dust in the upper boundary load was not sufficient, which was due to under performance of the passages of the conveyor screws. Even so, steam generation remained more or less unsatisfactory, though fire space temperatures were consistently high.

A small result that the author had after returning from a test drive was supposed to bring the beginning of a turnaround. At the junction to the locomotive assembly shop of the Ashford Railway Works, the head of the same, Mr. Pearson, awaited the machine. According to our report, he shook his head. 'I never see your machine smoking,' he said, 'Let the machine smoke, and you will see what steam they have.'

On 26 November 1930, the outbound journey was carried out again in the usual way. 'Think of Mr Pearson's words,' the pilot admonished on the drive home. Halfway through, the safety valves lifted and remained so until Ashford, despite both injectors being full on.

The cinder image gave us an answer to the question of why. Two flame paths had become clear: the path from the outbound journey and the way of the return journey, when the road was driven with higher pressure but also with higher dust production. The cinder coating on the brick arch of the firebox largely showed coal entry. The analysis of the smokebox char (six heating chamber scars full) showed 19.4% in ash and 77.4% in fixed carbon in 2.8% volatile components. From this analysis and from the cinder results, the cylinder power had been obtained with the help of the volatile components in the coal, while the fixed carbon flew almost unburned out to the chimney. So dust firing had become more or less 'gas firing.'

As a result, the test drives were continued in this direction, albeit with varying results, albeit at the unfortunate protest of the station staff of Ashford station, who complained strongly about pollution from the test train by fly ash. It was therefore attempted to use the installation of a screen in the smokebox and to retain a so-called 'baffle-plate'. But firing with the dust conveyor almost at the maximum limit led to the fact that the evaporation rate soon showed a declining trend again. While the performance required has now been achieved, the loss of unburned dust could not be overlooked. The cause of the poor combustion is likely to be found mainly in the narrow fire box situated between the frames. The fly ash problem, which could not be completely remedied even after the installation of the 'baffle-plate' prompted the Southern Railway to abandon the tests in 1931.

Slip Coaches on the Chatham and South Eastern

David Austin

One train service into two

The early railways were much hampered by the availability of sufficient motive power for their train services and from the limited number of routes into

SER rolling stock and porters circa 1885. We make no excuses: finding images to accompany this piece has been 'challenging'. The editor apologies for the limited number but also thanks Mike King for coming to the rescue at the eleventh hour.

London. The operational solution was to divide trains outside the metropolis and despatch them to different destinations, thereby reducing pressure on the dependency of engines and route paths. A variation of the stop and divide procedure was to slip coaches off the back of a train at speed to achieve the same aim of train division. Slipping gave significant benefits by reducing the need to stop the fast-running express trains.

Third-brake No. 3311 built at Ashford in 1908 and at the time SEC No. 969. The droplight for the guard remains in this 1949 view, although the slip coupling has long been replaced by a standard fitting. *Denis Cullum*

This saved time on services that were often tightly timed. When a slip coach is detached from the original train it can be formed into another train to be taken forward or terminated at the station of detachment. At the end of slip services in the mid-1920s, the South Eastern had developed a schedule of slipping coaches off express trains and making these 'all stations stopping trains' that terminated at the same destination as the express.

Slipping into folklore

The railwaymen of past generations have always subscribed to the idea that slip coaches came about from an incident that occurred in the days before continuous brakes came into general use. The story goes that a high railway official, wishing to travel to a certain important junction, went to the terminus to catch his train. It so happened that there was a train at either side of the platform; the train on the left was a non-stop express, and that on the right a fast train but which called at several of the principal stations, including the one at which the official wanted to alight. He did what thousands of other railway travellers have done, and probably always will do – boarded the wrong train, and did not find out his error until the express passed through several stations at which the other train

was booked to stop. He had just resigned himself to a weary journey back on a 'local', when, to his astonishment, his carriage began to slow down and finally stopped at the platform of the junction that was his intended destination. His surprise was nothing to the shock he received when he alighted and found that the rest of the train had disappeared altogether, excepting the solitary carriage in which he had travelled.[1]

So from an accidental slip in folklore to the well-documented coach slipping by design. The London & Greenwich Railway (LGR) was opened for public service on 8 February 1836. The line was planned to run from Greenwich through Deptford to London Bridge as the first ever railway terminus in the inner sanctum of the greatest city in the world. It was for that reason it was destined to become a very famous railway, but there was a little known hiccup along the way.

The key feature of the line, and the reason why it was allowed to be built at all, was that the route was elevated upon an engineering masterpiece of a viaduct made up of millions of bricks. The huge expense of this ground-breaking infrastructure addressed the problems of laying railway lines through areas of population and also prepared the railway to cross the Thames at a height such as to clear the masts of ships – but see below. Of course, the normal method of laying tracks is to level the road as much as possible on a series of embankments and cuttings but the impact of an embankment through a highly populated area was that the railway would effectively divide the residents into isolated pockets of people regardless of community boundaries. Consequently, there was much local opposition to schemes that aimed to project new railways into the metropolis due to the fear of the virtual imprisonment of the residents. *(Early NIMBY's – Ed!)*

(Note: It is true that elevating the line on a viaduct, prepared the railway for crossing a river at high level, but with the possible exception of the High Level Bridge over the Tyne, a ship's mast would not clear it as even the smallest coasting ketch had a masthead height of some 40ft. But just as steam was the power for the railway, so it was for the coasting trade from 1900 onwards and for tug boats that towed shipping to the up-river wharves – and tugs had funnels that could be lowered, and we had the 'flat-iron' colliers that supplied the Thames-side power stations, and could 'crawl' under the bridges when the tide's height was right.)

The pioneering edifice of LGR used new techniques to build a 22ft-high brick viaduct on concrete foundations in marshy ground. With 851 arches and twenty-seven bridges and over three and three quarter miles long, the passengers enjoyed the vista of a cityscape from the cramped and uncomfortable carriages. But at least the open arches of the viaduct gave the local residents a good chance of living as normal a life as possible. This remarkable engineering achievement was to prove to be a template for future London and other inner city railways. Unfortunately, the last section of line on the approaches to London Bridge station could not be completed in time for the grand opening. The double line track work stopped abruptly at the chasm of Bermondsey Street for the want of an iron bridge, which was being forged at Dudley. Consequently, a temporary wooden station was set up at Spa Road to allow passengers to disembark from the train and to continue their journey to the city.

The northbound and southbound lines on the narrow viaduct at this impromptu halt could not provide for the release of locos on the London-bound trains. A temporary movement operation was needed for this temporary station so that the promise to start the service could be upheld. Accordingly, the northbound train was attached to its locomotive by a length of rope by a 'hook rope man'. As the train approached the wooden platforms of Spa Road station, the points were set up for a cross over to the southbound line. The loco hit the points and veered off the northbound line. The guard lifted the rope coupling off the leading coach and the police (points) man reversed the points. The train of coaches then continued northwards until brought to a halt in the station by the guard using the coach handbrake. In the meantime, the loco gently buffered up to the southbound train ready for its departure to Deptford. The railway company thoughtfully provided some large blocks of stone to act as buffer stops to prevent coaches and occupants from continuing towards London and being dashed onto the pavement of the high street.[2]

The railway was a great success in that it was well served by commuters who wished to escape the even more sordid hell of an overcrowded horse omnibus service offered by George Shillibeer. The bus company, as well as the water ferries, was put out of business soon after the railway started and Shillibeer himself suffered a double whammy when he, and a party of passengers walking along the track in the pitch darkness of an unlit night, fell into the pit formed by the temporary absence of ballast at Bermondsey High Street. He was awarded £25 in damages.[3]

However, it appears that the slipping operation was generally successful with the exception of an incident in January of 1837 when the pointsman was absent, a locomotive derailed and the following carriages collided with it.[4]

The practice continued into 1840, as evidenced by an accident report dated 30 January where a Croydon train arrived later than scheduled at Corbett's Junction due to thick fog. It joined the line towards London Bridge but was out of sequence behind a Greenwich train. When the latter stopped to put on the (slip) rope, the Croydon train ran into the back of it, causing remarkably little damage. Unfortunately a second Greenwich train appeared upon the scene and crashed into the wreckage giving more damage but luckily without injury.[5]

The fly shunting of wagons has long been a useful tool in the railway operations' manual, but this practice of slipping of passenger coaches was also noted on the London & Croydon Railway at the time where the operatives were called 'Tail Rope Men'. Nevertheless, the practice of slipping passenger vehicles from these early days in 1836 on the London & Greenwich was to become an essential part of a drive to achieve performance efficiencies in the face of intensive competition from other companies in the early 1900s.

Using slips as needs must

The LB&SCR is recognised as being the first company to design and build a specialised slip coach. The service to introduce slipping coaches started in February 1858 to Hastings, for which a coach was slipped at Haywards Heath from a London–Brighton express.[6]

Later in that year the slips on GWR expresses were detached at Slough and Banbury. Then in 1869, on the Bristol and Exeter Railway – later, part of the Great Western – the 'Flying Dutchman' began the practice of slipping a coach at Bridgwater. Since then the GWR has always been partial to the device and eventually accommodated the greatest number of daily slip services.

The GER used slip carriages in 1872 and from the 1890s was second only to the GWR in the number; in the order of nineteen per day, including four at Tottenham, four at Colchester and two each at Broxbourne, Audley End, Brentwood and Chelmsford, plus one each at Bishop's Stortford and Marks Tey. These had, however, been abandoned by 1901, leaving the GER Main line (at Marks Tey) to be the last user up until just before the Second World War.[7]

Before 1914, twenty-one coaches were slipped each day on the London–Brighton main line. Coaches were detached at Horley and Three Bridges for stations to East Grinstead, Forest Row and Horsham, or at Haywards Heath for stations to Brighton and Eastbourne. The practice continued until electrification of the Brighton main line in 1932.[8] *(See SW42 containing an article and illustrations of slipping on the Brighton line in SR days.)*

The slip workings were brought back at the cessation of hostilities in 1918 and continued up to the start of the Second World War. Later the GWR was the only company to reintroduce slip carriage workings after the war and its successor, BR-WR, was running slip services until as late as Friday, 9 September 1960.

To slip or not to slip

There has always been, in railway operations, a long-standing practice of dividing trains at points along the route and working through coaches forward to their final destinations. However, the effort in stopping a fast, heavy, mainline express train and then restarting it consumes time, coal, and imparts much wear on the machinery and train crew. The slip coach is a neat way of minimising the effort to separate it from the main train and allows the company to provide services to branch line stations with fast mainline trains. When detached from the express at an intermediate station on the main line, the slipped coach is taken into a branch line train and continues to its final destination or is shunted into sidings for a return journey.

There are several benefits for the railway in saving time on express services, some of which may be carrying mails under a lucrative contract that require delivery on time. The company also reduces the route miles for the branch line train and the cost of its crew. At the peak of the slipping services in the summer of 1914, there were 177 daily slips by the main railway companies, so the practice clearly had benefits in a number of ways. And we must not forget that in the early days of the railways there was a severe shortage of motive power at all levels of train service operations. The use of slipping coaches was an effective method of reducing route miles and combining branch line services with mainline express speeds. There was though the need and cost to build specially fitted coaches and to train slip guards, but these costs must have been relatively small compared with capturing market share and reducing costs elsewhere.

Slip systems and operations

To detach a coach from a live running train at speed required some consideration and two systems have been found to be used. The vehicles of a train are physically connected by couplings on the drawbar and with inter-carriage services through flexible pipes. The latter include air and/or vacuum brakes, steam and intercommunications. When the vehicle is separated these services have to be isolated at each side of the break point so that both portions of the train can continue to operate as independent units. The solution for the GWR was a flap valve in the brake line within the last train vehicle. As the slip coach released and slowed down, a pin attached to the slip coach was pulled out of a flap valve in the train brake line, allowing a flap to drop down and to seal the line. The LNER design had a plug valve in the connector of the flexible brake pipe that was closed by the guard prior to releasing. The action of pulling a cord closed the valve on the slip side and automatically closed a valve on the train side of the flexible pipes. The LNER also used a locking shackle on the coupling that was released by the slip

guard pulling a cord. On the GWR this same effect was achieved by removing a pin on a drawbar hook that then rotated to allow the train coupling to drop free.

The operating instructions for most companies follows a common procedure:

The guards on the train and the slip prepare for the release by checking that there is sufficient vacuum in the brake and that they are both ready to release.

The slip guard observes the distant signal on the approach to the station where the release is scheduled and if it is clear then operates the release lever. Otherwise the train is to stop at the station with the slip still attached.

The brake valves are sealed on both train and slip portions and other disconnections made.

The coupling release is operated and a brake application made to distance the slip from the train.

Upon a successful clean release, the slip guard signals to the train guard, who communicates to the driver.

The slip guard controls the speed of the coach so as achieve no more than 20mph at the entry to the station platform. The coach is brought to a halt at the platform. The slip has additional vacuum reservoirs to allow for up to four brake applications.

Slips on the South Eastern and Chatham Railway (SE&CR)

The subject of slipping coaches was discussed in an article entitled 'Slipping Coach Services' for the SE&CR Society journal, *Invicta*, where the late Malcolm Parker noted that in 1909 only five slips were operated by the SE&CR out of a total of 146 slipping services on all of the major railways.[9]

Reported as the new Ashford carriage shop, c.1870.

In the rush of Railway Mania in the latter half of the nineteenth century there were many lines and services being promoted in an avalanche of bills being submitted to Parliament. Several notable members remarked that the value of these schemes far exceeded all of the gold in the country many times over. So it was that the Chatham proposed in 1857 a new route from Faversham to Herne Bay. It would provide the coastal town with a faster train and horse bus service to the same place. Upon the opening of the Chatham (London, Chatham & Dover Company) service in 1861 the SER proposed to address the threat of intense competition by providing a slipping service at the previously unknown halt at Sturry and by charging cheaper fares.[10]

The late Roger Kidner recorded that the SER had made 'considerable use' of slips, with the first noted in May 1858 at Canterbury off the 12.30 London Bridge to Ramsgate. In 1861 there was a slip at Caterham for Reading and Maidstone.[11]

The L&G may have carried the mails under contract since the opening of their line in 1842 but under the ownership of the South Eastern the India Mails contract had to be conveyed through the new military port of Dover so as to protect the maritime assets of the mail ships. The SER had developed Folkestone Harbour in 1843 as the point of departure for their new cross-channel business and Continental Express service. Accordingly, in 1862 the SER relinquished the mails service to the up and coming Chatham which was laying lines towards Dover from the north of Kent.[12]

With the important mail contract secured, the Chatham's Continental Mail express train in 1873 was running from Victoria to Dover on a very tight timetable. This was a prestige, initially first-class only, express train that ran twice a day in both directions. For years it was hauled by 'Europa' class (2-4-0 tender) locomotives specially designed to ensure fast, reliable running. The mails consisted of two vans and four passenger coaches, and were fitted with Westinghouse air brakes for the first time on the Chatham. The trains were built to be fast and reliable to keep the mail contract and the service is thought to have contributed much in saving the company from bankruptcy. This was the train that allowed individuals to leave their London home in the morning, have lunch in Paris with a business partner and get back to London by midnight. (again, see note) The Continental Mail trains were complemented by magnificent, and very fast, cross-Channel paddle steamers built specially for the Mails contract.[13]

(Note: Yes in theory it was possible and we may suspect a bit of slight 'spin' in what is said. 'If' you could get to Paris in under eight hours, door to door in 1873 – always allowing sensible lengths of time, for two transfers from train to boat and boat to train, then that left you with twenty minutes for lunch with your friend in Paris. From the time you leapt out of the train at the Gare du Nord – and assuming you went no further than the station restaurant, and that your friend had pre-ordered the meal – you actually had about ten minutes to eat your lunch before you sprinted back to catch the return service.)

The formation of the Mails in 29 November 1875 consisted of six-wheeled vehicles, being Brake van No. 39, composite 17, first 167, second 70, first 163, and brake van 17. Bradley informs us that a slip carriage was attached to the rear of the 7.40 am down Continental Mails express to be detached at Chatham for the convenience of Naval officers and officials visiting the Royal Dockyard. It was returned later in the morning in time to provide Chatham with a second fast service off the 4.20 pm Victoria–Dover express. The Chatham slip carriage was composite No. 35 and for more than a decade its daily travels were given special mention in the company's working timetables.[14]

The Chatham slips started in September of 1872 when the 5.15 pm service from Victoria slipped at Swanley to be worked forward as a slow service to Chatham. This slip was replaced later in the same year with a slip at Chatham off the 4.20 pm Victoria service, which continued to 1899. There were also slips at Beckenham between 1873 and 1881, and at Faversham from 1890 to 1926.[15]

The early Chatham slips were 28ft long, six-wheel, composite brake vehicles from 1891 to 1896. As the six-wheelers were being withdrawn at the end of the century, the joining of the Chatham with the South Eastern meant that former did not need to replace the slips with bogie vehicles. To fill the gap, the SE&C built five-bogie slip coaches in 1909 to Drawing 25, being bogie Slip Brake Composite Lavatory vehicles with 50ft 1in body length. These were numbered 976–980 and upon grouping renumbered to 6637–6641. The normal slip coach layout was (from the slip end): birdcage/guard, luggage, first, lavatory, first, lavatory, second, second, lavatory. In 1911 the SE&C converted three of the 50ft Birdcage Lavatory Brake thirds – Nos 852, 968/9 – into slip coaches. There is evidence that other coaches were converted as coaches 824 and 853 were also noted as being slip fitted.

The SE&C formed train sets for the slip portions and set number 16 was allocated to the 7.55 am up service, Ramsgate Harbour to Charing Cross. This set then became the slip portion on the 5.10 pm service from Holborn Viaduct to Ramsgate and was detached at Faversham for all stations to Ramsgate. Set 16 was composed of Slip Brake Composite Lavatories 978 and 979, 3rd lavatory 869, and composite 2375. These vehicles were rotated out of service in the summer of 1909 to have heating fitted at Ashford but were replaced with the same type of coaches.

At this time SE&C bogie coach No. 231, a 44ft non-gangwayed corridor composite, was formed in set 29 to join the six-wheeled Slip Brake composite 2063, composite 3450 (a 44ft bogie coach built in 1900), six-wheel six-compartment thi3d 567, and six-wheel Brake Van No. 8. This set was reformed in 1915 with sister coach 234 replacing 231.[16]

There were also several prestige trains with the following examples. The 'Cliftonville Express' was introduced to the travelling public in October 1911 and scheduled to depart Victoria at 9.10 am to run non-stop to Ramsgate, arriving there at 11.02 am. A slip portion was detached at Faversham and became an all stations stopping train to Ramsgate Harbour. This service continued to operate after the coal strike in 1921 and with the added benefit of a Pullman tea car inserted into the formation in February 1922. The Faversham slip portion consisted of a slip coach and a trio set of three coaches. The service was still timetabled in September 1925 when a Dover portion was detached during a stop at Chatham.[18]

In June 1913 the 'Pullman Limited' express service was upgraded (or demoted) by the addition of third-class cars and renamed the 'Eastbourne Sunday Limited Express'. The train departed from Victoria and slipped a portion at Haywards Heath for the coastal town of Worthing.[19]

Another famous express with a slip component was the Sundays only 'Thanet Pullman Limited', which started service in July 1921. It departed Victoria at 10.10 am and ran non-stop to Ramsgate Harbour via Margate West with an 'E1' class heading a train that comprised Pullman cars *Sorrento*, *Ruby*, *Topaz*, *Leghorn*, *Daphne*, *Corunna* and a brake van. In the winter months the train was combined with an ordinary service that had a slip at Faversham for an all stations stopping service to Ramsgate.[21]

The 'Granville Express' had originally comprised set 10 and this was then renumbered to set 24. Its final composition was slip brake composite 978, 1st 939, composite 2375 and third lavatory 866, and it was disbanded in 1919. Train set 81 was comprised a slip and three coaches, and was disbanded in 1918.[22]

The passenger carriage slip services were suspended for the course of the Great War and then reinstated on 16 June 1919, but an unusual application of slip working, this time involving locomotives during the hostilities, has been recorded by Bradley. At the start of the war, the length of trains increased dramatically and getting these heavy trains over the long grades to the Kentish Weald became a major problem. The SE&C 0-6-0 tender goods locos of the 'O' class were paired with or piloted by Wainwright's 'C' class or 'O1s' to bank the heavy goods trains. Five members of the O class, Nos. 392, 393, 433, 435, and 436, were fitted with slip gear and sent to Tonbridge in 1915 to be the bankers for the route over the 'Kentish Weald' and the long grades over the North Downs. The slip coupling only was necessary and was able to be released from the footplate, so saving much time in keeping the war materials moving.[23]

The Kirtley design of 4-4-0 'M3' class locomotives were generally reckoned to be the best of their type. Just before the withdrawal of the last pair in 1928, the solitary example at Maidstone East was LDCR No. 192 (SE&CR 651) and this engine normally headed up the 7.20 am service to Holborn Viaduct. This was a well-patronised service and the heavy train included a portion of several carriages for Victoria. A slip was made at Herne Hill at 9.24 am, which then departed for Victoria at 9.27 am. The slip arrived at Victoria at 9.35 am, while the front half arrived at Holborn Viaduct at 9.38 am.

New SER brake-third No. 2294 (non-slip) at Ashford.

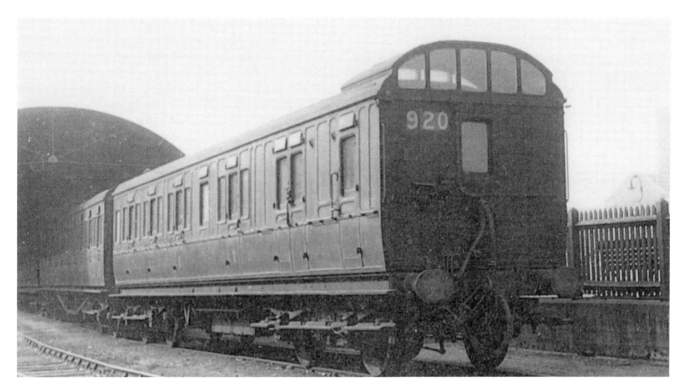

Another former slip vehicle: this had originally been No. 976 when built in 1909 but was renumbered 6637 by the Southern Railway in 1928. In its non-slip guise it was now part of set No. 920 at Maze Hill in September 1956. *H.C. Casserley*

The 5.10 pm 'Granville Express' down service was reputed to be the fastest train on the Chatham, being booked ninety minutes for 74 miles and requiring an average of 74½mph. (74 miles in ninety minutes is an average of 49.6mph: 74½ is getting on to 'Cheltenham Flyer' speeds, and while drivers such as Sammy Gingell could make an 'E1' go, the idea of taking the curves at the foot of Sole Bank at that sort of speed would scare the **** out of anyone.)

The train was headed by LCDR 'M3' No. 187 (SE&CR 646) from Holborn Viaduct and was non-stop from St Pauls and Margate. Carriages were slipped at Faversham to form a stopping train to Ramsgate, while a connection left at 6.28 pm to Dover Harbour that was timed to arrive there (at 7.28 pm) one hour before the competing SER service. [24]

It is worth noting that some slips had more than one vehicle in the slip portion and by inspecting the timetables we can see that in the slip services at Faversham. In the following table, the slip coach is identified as the TBD (Third Brake Detaching), and the numbers represent the coaches in the train and slip portions:

The summer timetable for 1922 had four regular slip services:

6.48 am Ashford–Cannon Street, then 1.25 pm Charing Cross–Deal with slip detached at Ashford.

8.20 am Ashford–Holborn Viaduct with slip detached at Herne Hill, then 2.13 pm Holborn–Swanley Junction where it was attached to the Victoria–Ashford train.

6.32 am Gillingham–Holborn Viaduct, then 5.31 pm Victoria–Faversham, slip detached at Swanley Junction to form the 6.15 pm to Gillingham.

9.47 am Gravesend West Street–Victoria, then 3.45 pm return, slip detached at Swanley Junction.

With the grouping and the reduced need for slipping services, the Swanley Junction and Herne Hill slips were discontinued in 1924 and the very last Faversham slip was detached in 1926. The actual slip coaches were reused in normal service trains being very distinctive and (as seen) were much sought after by photographers for many more years.[25]

Service	Train + Slip portions	Commentary
6.40 pm Faversham to Dover Marine	2 + TBD + 1	The TBD+1 were slipped from the 5.10 pm Holborn – Margate
6.12 pm Cannon Street to Ramsgate Harbour, first stop Margate West	7 + TBD + 2	This was a high-speed slip at Faversham A's outer home signal
7.28 pm Faversham to Ramsgate	4 + TBD + 2	The TBD + 2 were slipped from the 6.12 pm Cannon St – Ramsgate

The *Railway Magazine* surveyed the state of affairs for the centenary of the railways in 1925 and produced a table showing the daily slip services for 1914 and 1925. Using information from the 1909 edition of the same magazine, an indication of the rise and fall of the slip as a service is obtained both as individual concerns and also when 'grouped':

Company	1909	1914	1925
GWR	70	70	43
LNER group total	19	19	4
GER	16	14	2
GCR	2	4	2
GNR	1	1	0
LMS group total	39	51	6
CR	11	10	0
MR	8	18	0
LYR	6	7	6
LNWR	14	16	0
FR	1	nk	nk
Irish	nk	8	6
SR group total	18	29	7
LBSCR	13	21	6
SECR	5	8	1
Totals	**146**	**169**	**60**

At the height of slip coach working in 1922 there were eight slips on SE&C routes: two each at Tonbridge, Ashford, Faversham and Folkestone Junction. For the 1924 service season the Tonbridge, Ashford and Folkestone Junction slip coaches were still marshalled into the trains but were not slipped, and the Faversham slip stopped at the end of the 1925–26 winter service. This was attributed by Henry Andrews in 1953 to the increasing difficulty of finding suitable workings for their return.

The Faversham slip operation of 1924 was the last SE&C slip service and was described in some detail by Henry Andrews in 1953:

> With exhaust throwing showers of Tilmanstone sparks high in the sky, whistle screaming, ross-pops roaring, the 6.12 am Cannon Street used to make an impressive sight as it ran away from its slip. It was a point of honour with the top link Margate men to be clear of the down starter before the slip showed up under the bridge. The passengers certainly got a wild and furious ride for their £18.18.0d a quarter (First Class Season, three months, Margate to City) – and – then the slip ran in. It was resplendent in light chocolate brown, white roofs and red roof boards which in letters of pure gold indicated: CITY EXPRESS, LONDON & KENT COAST (FAVERSHAM SLIP).'

With the approved '2 pause 2' on the klaxon to say the slip was now at rest under the protection of fixed signals, the guard descended from his TBD to the

Vehicle 6637 at Blackheath. All the former slip vehicles appear to have had their slip gear removed around 1927–29. *Lens of Sutton*

platform. Even at the same level as ordinary men he was great, for had he not divided a train at speed and brought its hundred or more passengers safely into Faversham station'. The SE&CR slip coaches are noted as Nos. 824, 852, 853, 967 and 968, with No. 969 as spare to cover breakdowns or special workings.

Accidents and mishaps

Despite the rather dubious nature of detaching railway coaches from trains travelling at speed, there is little evidence of any serious accidents involving slip coaches. In our modern world under the protective scrutiny of health and safety we could be forgiven for thinking that the practice is dangerous and unwarranted, but in reality the railway companies were no less concerned about passenger safety in the early 1900s than they are now. We should remember that railway vehicles are designed to ride the rails at the certified speed of the train. The slip operation to detach the coach was carried out by a specially trained guard using a release mechanism developed for that action. The carriage is contained on the rails and is brought to a controlled stop under the supervision of the guard. It is difficult to see where any sort of danger would present itself from the slip coach as a free-running vehicle. Indeed, the following investigation report is the only evidence of slip operations causing an injury accident that has been found – and then away from the 'Southern':

On 19 Dec 1936, the LNER 6.20 pm express to Bradford was on the London to Leicester line with though coaches for Finmere and Stratford on Avon. The train consist was an 'Atlantic' type loco No. 6086 with a six-wheeled tender, seven-bogie corridor coaches, and two non-corridor slip coaches. The first slip coach was detached at Finmere without problem. At about 7.45 pm on a fine day the Stratford-upon-Avon coach was prepared to be slipped as scheduled at Woodford and Hinton. It was noted that the speed of the train was 70 mph to satisfy the need to match the schedule timing for the section.

After the slip coach was detached the main train unfortunately stopped suddenly so that the slip ran into the back of it. The slip coach over-rode the buffers of the last coach in the main train, causing both to telescope. The train guard and the slip guard were both seriously injured, and 11 other passengers suffered shock and minor injuries. The investigation found that the vacuum brake shut off valve on the train side had not sealed properly upon release so that the train brakes were applied automatically. There was discussion on the reason for this failure and the investigating officer, Lt Col E. Woodhouse, noted that the last coach in the train had non-standard fittings to suit a Pullman corridor connection. In respect of the actions of the train driver and the slip guard it was

No. 6637 at Maze Hill on 19 September 1956. *H.C. Casserley*

found that the driver should have whistled for the slip to apply brakes when the train slowed, even though he had not intentionally applied the train brakes. The slip guard had followed the correct procedure for detaching by observing that the distant signal for Woodford was off, that there was a vacuum in the slip coach when the brake pipes had been separated, and that upon releasing the slip shackle a momentary brake application had slowed the slip to slow sufficiently for it to clear the train. The guard had controlled the slip to about 20 mph to enter the station, but as his view of the rear of the train was obscured by steam, it was not possible to see that the train was slowing to a stop as well. The investigating officer noted that incidents involving slip coaches were very rare even though there were 150 slips per day in the pre-war (WWI) years. The practice had diminished considerably in recent years with the GWR having 20 slips per day and the LNER with just the two slips noted in this report. The LNER had, since February 1935, removed slip coach working and substituted stops at the stations to divide through coaches. The mechanism of the slip gear for the LNER differs from that of the GWR and the report recommended that the latter system would appear to be the more reliable and should be adopted by all companies.[26] (The editor has, somewhere, a similar report of an incident involving a failed GW slip at Bath/Chippenham but not relevant to include.)

The last slip

To give some idea of how important slipping was at one time, the number of slipping services increased from 146 in 1909 to 177 in 1914, of which 70 were on the GWR. By 1919 though there were three companies indulging in slip coaches, the GWR, the Lancashire & Yorkshire and the SECR. The GWR was slipping on seventeen trains, the L&Y were slipping five and the SECR on four. All the SECR slips were taken over by the Southern and discontinued during the 1920s,[27] although one at least SR service continued into the next decade – as previously mentioned.

On 30 April 1932 it is recorded that the last surviving slip coach made its last slip on the Southern Railway. The 5.05 pm express from London Bridge to Eastbourne conveyed the last slip, which was detached at Horley for Forest Row.[28]

In the early 1950s there were still about a dozen slip coach services each day on former GWR lines, serving such destinations as Didcot and Reading (from up trains) and Westbury, Taunton, Princes Risborough and Bicester (from down trains). Gradually, they were replaced by additional calls by expresses, until by 1959, only one such working survived which was discontinued in September 1960.

As an aside, the *Cornish Riviera*, which was also the longest non-stop train for many years, slipped a coach for Westbury before Heywood Road Junction right through to the late 1950s. This was done at a speed at about 70–80mph. The *Riviera* continued on the Westbury avoiding line and the single coach came to rest, after which the route was reset and a pilot engine coupled up to pull the coach into Westbury – no changing the points between the main train and slip in the 1950s! The service, in its winter formation, had two slip portions, detached respectively at Westbury and Taunton. At one time in its career it had three slip portions, the third being detached at Exeter.[29]

Up until 1953 the 8.30 am from Plymouth and the 8.20 am from Weston-super-Mare were also seen slipping at Reading at 20mph. The whole train would be sent through the Up Main Platform (No. 5) Loop and at that speed the guard did not pull his lever until he was just on the platform end.

Conclusion

And so, 120-plus years after the first slip on the L&G, the need and the desire for slipping coaches from moving trains has passed. In this age of unit trains, permanently coupled together, offering fast reliable services on a network greatly simplified and reduced in reach, the only competition is with road and air travel. The passing of an era of an independent railway operation was probably not mourned by the companies, but the spectacle of seeing railway trains freewheeling down the track to stop in a station must have been a unique experience. Certainly the authors of such antics, the slip guards, were publicly feted for their feats of skill and precision.

Bibliography and References

1. *Railway Wonders of the World* – 21 June 1935, p.655.

2. Thomas, *London's First Railway*, London & Greenwich, 1972, p.52.

3. Thomas, *London's First Railway*, London & Greenwich, 1972, p.82.

4. Thomas, *London's First Railway*, London & Greenwich, 1972, p.104.

5. Thomas, *London's First Railway*, London & Greenwich, 1972, p.116.

6. Ellis, 1979, pp.98–99.

7. www.lner.info/forums/viewtopic.php?f=5&t=8843&start=15.#

8. Gray (1977) p.87–97.

9. 'Model Railways and Locomotives April 1909', Malcolm Parker, SECSoc Invicta 1992, p.31.

10. Bradley, *Locos of LCDR*, RTCS 1979, p.5.

11. Kidner, *The SE&C Railway*, Oakwood, 1983, p.23.

12. POST 51/63 Contracts Post Master General, PRO.

13. *Slip Coaches at Chatham*, Kent History Forum, Sentinel 4. Henry Andrews 1924. Various contributors.

14. Bradley, *Locos of LCDR*, RTCS 1979, p.69.

15. Kidner, *The SE&C railway*, pp.93–94.

Opposite: **No. 6641 at an unknown location.**
Phil Coutanche courtesy Mike King

16. Gould, *Bogie Carriages of SE&CR*, pp.68–69.

17. Gould, *Bogie Carriages of SE&CR*, p.132.

18. Winkworth, *Southern Titled Trains*, pp.141–143.

19. Winkworth, *Southern Titled Trains*, p.110.

20. Winkworth, *Southern Titled Trains*, p.146, 148.

21. Winkworth, *Southern Titled Trains*, p.155.

22. Gould, *Bogie Carriages of SE&CR*, p.66.

23. Bradley, *Locos of SER*, p.83.

24. Bradley, *Locos of LC&DR*, p.115.

25. Gould, Bogie Carriages of SE&CR, p.146.

26. Lt Col E. Woodhouse, MoT Accident report, LNER Woodford and Hinton, 23 Mar 1936.

27. *The Railway Magazine*, 1925 Centenary, p.214.

28. *The Railway Magazine*, Jan–June 1932, vol. 70, p.460.

29. *Railways of the World*, June 1935, p.775.

30. Gould, *Bogie Carriages of SE&CR*, p.121.

31. HMRS drawings 1946, 22767/93/97.

References:

South Eastern & Chatham Society, *Invicta*:

P. Clark, 'Detaching vehicles', 1976, vol. 8 p.33.

I. Lyle, 'Detaching vehicles – bogie and 6 wheel types', 1976. vol. 8 p.33.

M. Parker, 'Slipping coach services', 1992, vol. 18 p.14.

J. Greaves, 'Slip working', 1999, vol. 53 p.56.

The grounded body of No. 3315 at Eastleigh sometime in the 1950s. This was to Diagram 51 and, according to Mike King, unique so far as its dimensions were concerned. *S. Clennell*

Irresistible Force/Immovable Object

Images From the Collection of Terry Cole

On 23 December 1955 an accident occurred on the down through line just east of Woking station when the 7.54 pm steam-hauled Waterloo–Basingstoke service ran into the rear of the 7.50 pm stationary Waterloo–Portsmouth electric unit – details of which EMU stock was involved are not given. Fortunately there were no fatalities, although twenty-one persons were injured. The Inspecting Officer, Col W.P. Reed, attributed blame to the driver of the steam engine No. 32327 *Trevithick* for missing the indication of the distant signal.

Although the impact speed was low, it was unfortunate that a few moments after the initial collision the late running 5.5 pm Bournemouth to Waterloo was passing on the up through line behind No. 34041 *Wilton*, although as the train had stopped at Woking this was fortunately at low speed. The rear bogie from the EMU had in consequence of the original collision been deflected sideways and this now proceeded to foul the 'six-foot', with the result that every outside axle box cover of the up train from the engine pony truck back – the tender and all eleven

coaches, were knocked off. The whole must have been a frightening experience for the crew and passengers on the Bournemouth service but the official report dismisses this with the words, 'An up passenger train ... scraped past the derailed bogie and was disabled by it, but was not derailed.'

As was customary for the time, normal services were quickly resumed, down steam trains passing after about two hours' interruption, although it was past midnight before up services were able to resume.

'Disabled' was certainly the word as two days later, on Christmas Day, the whole of No. 34041's ensemble was still immobile and awaiting engineers' attention.

We have no idea as to the original photographer – perhaps somebody who did not enjoy Christmas – as the album containing these views (none unfortunately of the damaged No. 32327 or EMU at the scene, although as services had been restored by the early hours of 24 December this is not surprising) was secured second-hand without any annotation as to the original owner/photographer.

It was in conversation with Terry on an unrelated issue that he suggested the incident might be of interest ... be assured Terry, it certainly is. Ed.

From the perspective of 'head-on' there appears to be little amiss, although the engine (and train) have already been cautiously moved to a siding off the main running lines.

Above: **From the side and it becomes a little more obvious – look at the bearing of the rear pony truck.**

A closer view of the same and now also with similar damage coming into view on the tender.

Close up of the pony truck and the leading axle of the tender. Part of the ashpan and the cab steps have also taken a bashing.

Now we see similar damage along and to the rear of the tender.

The first van from the train, recorded as No. 267. Our photographer did not record the rest of the stock – perhaps he had a Christmas dinner waiting after all!

Finally, the recalcitrant No. 32337, seen here at Eastleigh on Saturday, 14 January 1956. It is from the same album so we may assume the same photographer. Not surprisingly, No. 32337 was condemned but No. 34041 survived and after a works visit re-entered traffic in February 1956.

Also by Crécy

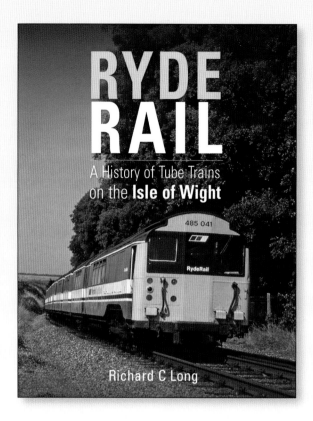

Ryde Rail
A History of Tube Trains
on the **Isle of Wight**

Richard C Long

One of the most interesting and unique parts of the national railway network is the line from Ryde to Shanklin on the Isle of Wight, which has been operated by former London Transport tube trains since the 1960s. *Ryde Rail* charts the history and operation of this line since the end of steam and the closure of most of the island's railway system in 1966. It follows the operation of the line in the decades since electrification to the present day and the changes which came about with privatisation of the national network.

While providing a history of this line, *Ryde Rail* also looks at its current and future operations, including the likely extension of the Isle of Wight Steam Railway trains to Ryde St John's.

This is a fascinating account of a unique survivor and perhaps the most singular line in the whole of the Britain's surviving railway network.

Hardback, 144 pages
ISBN: 9781910809570 **£20.00**

Crécy Publishing Limited
1a Ringway Trading Estate, Shadowmoss Road, Manchester M22 5LH
www.crecy.co.uk

Also by Crécy

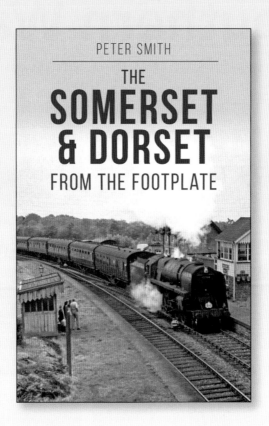

Somerset and Dorset
from the Footplate

Peter Smith

In the 1980s the Oxford Publishing Company produced an amalgam of two books written by former Branksome fireman Peter Smith entitled *Mendips Engineman* and *Footplate over the Mendips*. They told the story of a young railway fireman and his driver Donald Beale working on the fabled Somerset & Dorset line.

Unavailable for over 30 years, the book has now been reprinted and comes with a new set of black and white images illustrating the remains of this much loved cross-country railway.

Somerset and Dorset from the Footplate encompasses not just ordinary workings, but also the early footplate experiences of driver Donald Beale, as well as the climax of Peter's own railway career, driving the very last northbound *Pines Express* in 1962.

This is a book to be savoured, readers will once again be enthralled by these tales of working trains over the Somerset & Dorset line.

Paperback, 224 pages
ISBN: 9781909328921 **£9.95**

Crécy Publishing Limited
1a Ringway Trading Estate, Shadowmoss Road, Manchester M22 5LH
www.crecy.co.uk

Southern Way

The regular volume for the Southern devotee
MOST RECENT BACK ISSUES

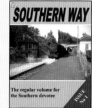

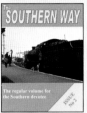
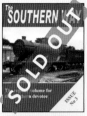

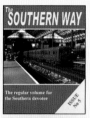

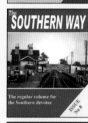

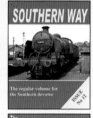

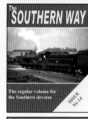
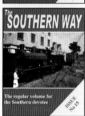

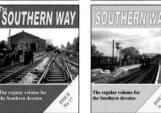

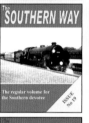
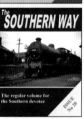
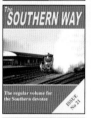
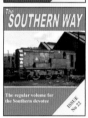

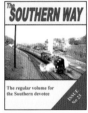

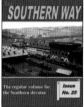
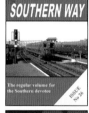
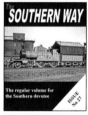
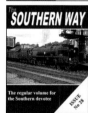
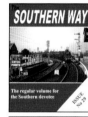

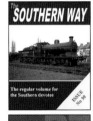

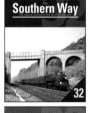
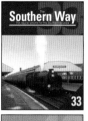
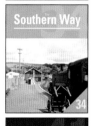
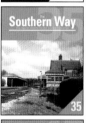
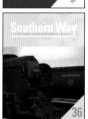

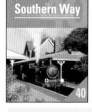
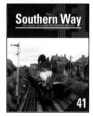
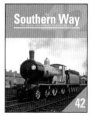
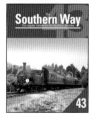

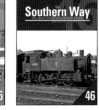

The Southern Way is available from all good book sellers, or in case of difficulty, direct from the publisher. (Post free UK) Each regular issue contains at least 96 pages including colour content.

£11.95 each
£12.95 from Issue 7
£14.50 from Issue 21
£14.95 from Issue 35

Subscription for four-issues available
(Post free in the UK)
www.crecy.co.uk